Recommen

The

Thira Edition

Praise for previous editions:

"The range of the accommodations recommended reflects the diversity of the islands themselves. Highly recommended to all variety of Caribbean travelers."
—*ALA Booklist*

"Strong . . . focuses mostly on the atmosphere of her subjects—their furnishings, surroundings and service . . . She points readers in the direction of appealing establishments, and lays the groundwork for further research . . . Introducing readers to a place they may grow to love is a worthy task indeed."
—*Caribbean Travel & Life, Summer Planner*

"Directs you to more than 150 charming historic inns and guest houses."
—*Los Angeles Times*

"If you're looking for an under-the-pillow book to provide exotic dreams, here it is."
—*The Charlotte Observer*

"Offers a selection of offbeat and charming accommodations in the islands, not all especially for families, but especially interesting. . . . Includes some charming alternatives to the big hotels of this part of the world."
—*Family Travel Times*

"More than 150 inns and guest houses are included in this selective guide, which emphasizes those places offering special touches."
—*Small Press*

Recommended
Island Inns ™
The Caribbean

Third Edition

by
Kathy Strong
Edited by Susan Farewell

A Voyager Book

The Globe Pequot Press

Old Saybrook, Connecticut

Previously published as *Bed and Breakfast in the Caribbean.*

Some of the illustrations and photographs in this book are reproduced with the permission of the establishment or representative. Special credit and appreciation are given to the following: Resorts Management, Inc.; Charela Inn, Jamaica; Caribbean Inns, Ltd.; La Casa del Francés, Puerto Rico; Blackbeard's Castle, U.S. Virgin Islands; Bunkers' Hill View Guest House, U.S. Virgin Islands; Fort Recovery Estate, British Virgin Islands; The Golden Lemon, West Indies; CPS Communications; Coccoloba, British West Indies; Mary's Boon, Netherlands Antilles; Hotel Frangipani, St. Vincent and The Grenadines; Vistalmar, Aruba; Salt Raker Inn, Grand Turk; Maison Greaux Guest House, St. Thomas; and Robert Strong.

Library of Congress Cataloging-in-Publication Data

Strong, Kathy, 1950–
    Recommended island inns : the Caribbean / by Kathy Strong. — 3rd ed.
        p. cm.
    Rev. ed. of: Bed and breakfast in the Caribbean. 2nd ed. c1987.
    "A Voyager book."
    Includes indexes.
    ISBN 1-56440-062-X
    1. Bed and breakfast accommodations—Caribbean Area—Guidebooks.
I. Strong, Kathy, 1950– Bed and breakfast in the Caribbean.
II. Title.
TX907.5.C27S77   1992
647.94729--dc20

                                                                92-5791
                                                                CIP

Manufactured in the United States of America
Third Edition/Second Printing

*To our Brent David,
whose spirit of adventure
makes traveling a special joy.*

Contents

Contents

Introduction

The Caribbean offers exotic beauty, sun-inspired recreation, and, perhaps above all, unparalleled diversity. In one relatively small geographic area lie several small groupings of islands referred to as the Caribbean, each group containing individual qualities that range from powdered-sugar beaches dissolving into crystal-clear turquoise waters to licorice and cotton candy-pink sands washed by deep-blue tides. The traveler will find old-world Danish villages and Las Vegas–type hotel and casino strips, as well as prim white colonial mansions and pastel-splashed Mediterranean bungalows clinging to mountainsides. These islands delight the traveler with volcanic peaks, waterfall-laden rain forests, and jungles draped in purple bougainvillea, hibiscus, and flamboyant, flat, arid cactus-sprouting desert and rolling hill pastures bathed in endless sunny days. But the diversity does not stop here.

The Caribbean is composed of many cultures, evolved from five centuries of rich history and reflected in varied languages, clothing, arts, religion, customs, architecture, and food. The traveler here can choose one or several of these multi-heritaged civilizations to experience, with the added promise that no more than thirty minutes away is a new world to explore.

For those adventurers who seek the genuine Caribbean—its people, its food, its way of life—there is no better way to visit these islands than by staying in those special, intimate spots that offer local hospitality and perhaps a slice of history. These are the inns and guest houses that are set apart from the plastic and neon, the spots that try hard not to hide their heritage or surroundings but instead invite the guest to sample their hospitality with personal, friendly service and to enjoy an intimate and individual stay. These special inns accomplish these goals in many ways that often include unique furnishings, such as island antiques and artwork, local foods prepared lovingly by the innkeeper, complimentary breakfasts, and many extra services not found in larger hotels.

The traveler to the Caribbean may choose from stays in historic inns such as a fifteenth-century guest house surrounded by acres of tropical gardens, a gingerbread-decorated Victorian overlooking a storybook village, or a converted sugar warehouse with cobblestone walkways, to name just a few. Or the visitor wanting a special stay might opt for a gracious inn or guest house built of locally quarried lava stone or white coral, an ancestral home filled with antiques, a working banana plantation decorated in rattan and *Casablanca*-style fans, or a simple yet congenial private residence with guest rooms.

This edition of *Recommended Island Inns: The Caribbean*™ (formerly *Bed & Breakfast in the Caribbean*) has been totally updated, reflecting the various changes in these unique lodgings as well as offering many new getaway spots on almost every island in the Caribbean.

Whether it be a historic inn, small hotel, or guest house, these individual offerings, both simple and elaborate, are all the same in several important ways. They are for the traveler seeking authentic, unique stays often overlooked by travel agents, and they feature innkeepers willing to share their knowledge of the area and their special form of hospitality. So go ahead—picture yourself sipping rum while sitting on a fragrant veranda, diving into a sparkling mountain spring–fed pool, sleeping in a massive four-poster in a former governor's mansion, eating stuffed breadfruit and mangoes fresh from the innkeeper's garden . . . all in the slow, intimate pace afforded by these special inns and guest houses of the Caribbean.

Part One

Exploring the Caribbean

The Caribbean: A Tourist Destination

The Caribbean is surely one of the most popular travel destinations of the world, and the tourist offices there are eager to help the visitor discover its many attractions and beauty. But what exactly constitutes the Caribbean? In this book and in many other presently dealing with this area, the Caribbean "tourist" islands are those generally referred to as the "West Indies." Therefore, terms such as "West Indian guest house" and "West Indian charm" are used almost interchangeably with "Caribbean." The West Indies are the islands that border the Caribbean Sea on both the east and north. These islands surrounded by warm, calm waters begin with Cuba and curve boomerang-style down to Trinidad and Tobago. Aruba and the Netherlands Antilles of the Caribbean are a reasonable jump away off the coast of Venezuela.

When to Travel to the Caribbean

One of the most agreeable details of planning a trip to the Caribbean is not having to worry about *when* you go. The traveler can choose almost any time of the year and still experience the idyllic warm days, tepid waters, and refreshing trade winds. Not many travel destinations can promise such a perfect situation, with year-round temperatures averaging about 80 degrees!

Since climate is not a major criterion for selecting a trip time, you may want to consider instead the factors of crowds and costs. If you want to avoid crowds in the stores and restaurants and on transportation and have the innkeeper's keener attention, as well as save up to 50 or 60 percent on room costs, then the Caribbean's generous off-season is for you. During this mid-April through mid-December period, the traveler can be more spontaneous in general and possibly save additional money on flights and/or cruises. Not only does the off-season traveler save money and hassles, but he or she also has a better chance of getting reservations in the small inn or guest house of preference. Also, many of the smaller establishments close during the months of September and October, so check carefully.

How to Get There

By Plane: Direct flights into the Caribbean from major U.S. and international cities go to all of the larger islands and many of the smaller ones. Flying is certainly the fastest way to get anywhere in the Caribbean, even when connecting flights are necessary to reach more remote destinations. The traveler will discover that flying is more ideally suited to visiting a particular island or a group of islands, but can become more complicated when trying to island-hop extensively. Island-hopping is possible with the aid of local airlines or small boats that ferry between islands, but it is something to be attempted without a rigid timetable and with a spirit of adventure. The commuter airlines that travel between islands can be an experience in themselves. You may find them surprisingly prompt, but often very small and informal. In order to gain entry to each of the islands in the Caribbean you must have a return or on-going ticket from that same island. Thus too casual an itinerary won't work. Some of the major airlines offer savings during off-season from certain cities. This can change with each new schedule, so it is advisable to have your travel agent check on any special discounts and the restrictions that may accompany them. Also have your travel agent check into reasonable charter flights as well as stopover flights on regularly scheduled airlines that may allow you to see two islands for the price of one. One other thing to remember about flying is that on some of the islands airport car rental agencies may close early. Be prepared to take a taxi and pick up your car the next morning if necessary.

Cruises and Yachts: Traveling via water has been a tradition in the Caribbean since the days of Columbus; the traveler may chose from a wide range of boating possibilities, from "barefoot" sailing to opulent "Love Boat" cruising. The more adventurous traveler might select a Windjammer with a fully trained crew or charter a boat that matches his or her level of expertise, with or without aid of a crew.

Of course, the luxury cruise lines offer a vast array of choices, including smaller or larger vessels and a choice of as few as two island stops in a week to as many as a dozen in a two-week period. The number of ports offered will give you an idea of the thrust of your trip—whether it is more ship-oriented or geared towards inport sightseeing. If the traveler wants to combine the experience of luxury cruising with a stay in the various Caribbean inns and guest houses, then a travel agent is the best bet for arranging a "land and sea" package. Note that cruising, like flying, to the Caribbean seems to be more competitive at present with an influx of more ships with more berths to fill; watch the ads carefully for discounts, especially when round-trip airfare is included.

Whether traveling by land or sea, do try to book your transportation as far ahead as possible; during on-season it is a must.

The Caribbean's Inns and Guest Houses: Variety, History, and Hospitality

Just as the islands of the Caribbean vary, so do each island's special offerings—its intimate inns and guest houses. Several centuries of colorful history since the first Europeans sailed into the Caribbean have yielded an abundance of preserved historical sites. The traveler here will also enjoy the contrasts: the modern among the very old and the creative and unique combinations of the various cultural influences and periods.

Architecture and Period

The inns and guest houses of the Caribbean are often prime architectural examples of well preserved history, having been converted through the years to overnight lodging establishments as well as restaurants and mini-resorts. Many times this conversion has taken place with great sensitivity to the inn's original use, its history kept intact for current generations to enjoy and experience. This sometimes translates into less modern amenities: shared baths, lack of air conditioning, less sophisticated plumbing systems, and so forth, but many of these historically preserved establishments have successfully blended the modern amenities with the past without sacrificing too much of the structure's original identity. The inns and guest houses in this publication include both types, all worth the experience. You have the rare opportunity to stay overnight in a nineteenth-century shipwright's home turned guest house, in a former Spanish consul's residence, in a 1780-built Danish townhouse, a 1650 plantation house, in cottages and suites built around the ruins of a seventeenth-century sugar mill, or in a 1788 dockyard storage warehouse constructed of giant ship beams and thick brick walls. Or you may want to stay in an English-style country house, in a romantic 1780 governor's mansion with twin gables, in a eighteenth-century coffee plantation home, in a gingerbread-decked Victorian, or on a working banana plantation situated on sixteen tropical acres.

For those seeking more modern facilities, the Caribbean islands also offer many family-run guest houses and homes with traditional West Indian ambience. Choose from a two-story residential-style villa with upper and lower verandas, a newly built bungalow, or a simple white stucco block home, to name just a few examples.

Size and Type

The inns and guest houses of the Caribbean range from simple to quite elaborate architecturally, and they also vary in size. However, they tend to be smaller and more intimate than comparable U.S. lodgings, and this accounts for the personal level of service they all offer. A small, family-run guest house may offer as few as two guestrooms, while some of the larger inns have nearly 100 units. But most of the establishments in this guide offer fewer than twenty rooms for guests, a quantity that lends itself well to the personal touches the inn-goer is seeking.

Furnishings and Accessories

The furnishings and accessories found in the guestrooms and common areas of these inns and guest houses range from design magazine showpieces to quite literally sparse; this variety is often reflected in the rates. Depending upon your traveling budget, needs, and preferences, you can choose from a wide selection of interesting, exciting, and culture-reflecting motifs. The two things that almost all these establishments have in common are uniqueness of decor, with every room and every inn a new experience, and an emphasis on comfort and cleanliness, even in the most modest.

Four-poster beds are also common in many of these intimate spots, especially those historical in nature; some are ornately hand-carved. Century-old French colonial beds, Victorian wicker, island and New England antiques, as well as handmade built-in furnishings, grace many of these inns and set off interior architectural detailings such as thick stone walls, cathedral-beamed ceilings, wood-paneling, and mahogany spiraling staircases. The floor coverings range from hand-painted tiles to flagstone, as well as very modern wall-to-wall carpeting.

Colors and fabrics in these often spacious, airy rooms are frequently coordinated and can be in colorful island fabrics or even chintz. Tropical print wallcoverings are common, as well as use of local art and tapestries. Special guestroom detailing might include a hand-quilted bedspread or French doors or a balcony leading out to a flower- and fruit-filled courtyard.

Settings

These Caribbean islands encompass mountains, beaches, forests, deserts, urban centers, and rolling countryside, all of which serve as settings for these intimate hostelries. The traveler will discover charming spots on tree-lined residential streets, in the heart of town, in the center of an operating cattle ranch, on a 700-acre estate that is also a bird and wildlife sanctuary, amid a rain-forested coffee plantation, and on a multitude of ocean- and beach-embracing sites.

The Extras

Factors other than furnishings and accessories commonly go into making your stay at these inns and guest houses warm and hospitable. These extra services performed by the innkeepers, as well as additional facilities, set these spots apart from the average hotel or motel.

Most of the inns and guest houses herein provide their guests with a common area for reading, socializing, or enjoying often complimentary afternoon tea or evening drinks. This common area might be a living room, drawing room, library, or veranda, but is usually stocked with reading material and comfortable furniture and sometimes music, television, or an honor bar. Outside, terraces offer spectacular views, sunbathing decks are designed for privacy, and patios and courtyards are the locales of meals and poolside lounging.

The recreation facilities go from a simple pool to mini-resort status. Among these inns and guest houses you will discover almost every kind of sport facility available in the Caribbean. Many have their own tennis courts or offer courts nearby; almost all have a swimming pool whether it be a fresh water, salt water, mountain spring-fed, free-form, or traditional pool. You'll find virtually every water sport offered on a loan or rental basis, including scuba and boating, with many spots possessing their own docks in case you arrive with a yacht of your own. Add to this horseback riding and breathtaking walks or hikes through tropical gardens, acreage, and plantations.

Guests at these special inns and guest houses are often offered use of the kitchen for storing groceries or even cooking. The innkeepers assist in many ways, including arranging sightseeing trips, providing free transportation to the beach, turning down the beds at night, and even polishing guests' shoes at the end of the day.

Breakfast and Other Meals

Many of the establishments in this guide offer a personalized stay combined with complimentary breakfast fare. Others offer breakfast at an additional charge, and a few inns offer no breakfast at all. However, most inns and guest houses herein do offer the morning meal in some form, and you'll be pleased at the variety you will find. The guest might enjoy breakfast on an outside veranda or private patio overlooking the ocean or surrounded by tropical gardens, in a gracious dining room with a table set in fine china, or in a homey parlor with homebaked breads and fresh fruit from the garden.

Lunches and dinners, when offered, are sometimes included in the rate and very often you'll be glad. Indeed, some of these establishments are renowned for their cuisine, another personal statement by the innkeeper. Rates fluctuate from modest to gourmet as do the dishes offered. Very European in nature, some of the inns in this guide consist of a few rooms above a highly revered eating establishment. Many local dishes are found on the menus, including a lot of fish and fresh vegetables, as well as some memorable French cuisine.

Reservations
and Other Concerns

Making Your Reservation

Reserving a room in your special inn or guest house need not be difficult just because you are many miles away in a different part of the world. All of the listings in this guide provide a mailing address, phone number, and, when available, toll-free phone numbers and/or a U.S. reservation representative. (Complete listings are in the back of this guide.) A reservation is a must in on-season and is a good idea in off-season because of the limited number of accommodations in many of these establishments. If you are to arrive on an island in the late evening, make every attempt to have a secured reservation in advance. There is nothing more frustrating than to begin searching for an overnight accommodation when you are tired and unfamiliar with your surroundings. This guide will give you an idea of distance from a particular establishment to the airport and/or public transportation when possible. Always book with a U.S. reservation agent, when provided, for speed and efficiency. If you are booking directly with the Caribbean innkeeper, allow for delayed mail each way and don't be surprised if a confirmation takes up to a month or more. Also, you may find that your innkeeper's response is less formal and more personal than you may be used to. If you choose to phone your selected inn for a reservation, you will find that the method of calling individual islands varies, even from area to area within the island itself. All of the islands in this guidebook provide phone service, and, by dialing 1 plus the area code 809 followed by the establishment's phone number, you may now dial directly to many of the islands. Some of the islands can be reached by dialing the international access code (011) plus the area codes 596, 590, 509, or 599 and then the local phone number. However, from some areas in the United States it is not possible to dial directly with an international access code; in those instances the operator will complete your call. Reaching some of the establishments in this book requires operator assistance.

To confirm a reservation you are usually required to send a deposit, normally the charge for the first night's stay or longer for on-season. When sending the deposit or asking for information, be sure to request the establishment's brochure, rate card, post card, and even menus when applicable. Do not be afraid to ask for advice or assistance, such as special dinner reservations or car rental information, and the like. This is one of the delightful benefits of staying in a small, intimate spot. Also, remember to notify your inn of your time of arrival, especially if it will be late, so that they will be prepared for your "homecoming."

When making your travel plans be sure to consult with your travel agent about time changes. The Caribbean islands in this guidebook have two separate time zones that equal Eastern Standard Time and Atlantic Standard Time, one hour later than Eastern Standard Time. However, only a few of the islands (Turks and Caicos, Cayman Islands, Jamaica, and Haiti) employ Daylight Saving Time (May through late October). During those months, the islands on Eastern Standard Time become an hour earlier than EST, and the islands on Atlantic Standard Time are in harmony with Eastern Daylight Time.

One word about staying at these inns and guest houses with children. Many are ideally suited for family situations; others are not, due to the intimacy of the inn or the fragile furnishings. Be sure to notify your innkeeper or the booking agent if reservations include a child to avoid any inconvenience or embarrassment. When meals are included in the stay, check to see if you must pay for a third person, fourth person, etc. to compensate for additional meals. Having traveled the Caribbean with a young child, I can attest that the Caribbean people are generally very loving toward small children and considerate of their needs, and your trip can be very rewarding family-style.

By the time you have gotten to know more about your selected inn and innkeeper and made your reservation, don't be surprised to be greeted like part of the family upon arrival. One innkeeper relates that it is difficult to charge her guests for the evening drinks they share because they are more like company than paying customers!

Special Concerns

Water: Most of the drinking water in the Caribbean has been chemically treated and is safe to drink, but it is different nonetheless. If you have an oversensitive system, you may want to try the water in small doses at first or request bottled water instead. Though surrounded by miles and miles of water these islands do have a fresh-water scarcity problem; a conscientious traveler here will use water carefully. Not only is water at a premium, but hot water is very precious—in fact, sometimes not offered at all. But this deficiency is less important than you might think. When the constant temperature ranges from 75 to 95 degrees, a cool shower could be quite welcome!

Shared Baths: Those very familiar with guest house and bed and breakfast travel in the United States and Europe have this topic well in hand; they know it isn't a problem. But for those of you who are hesitant about sharing a bath, you may choose from many establishments in this guide that offer private facilities or you might like to be adventurous and give the bath "down-the-hall" a try. What you'll discover is that there is rarely any inconvenience involved with the usual small ratio of sharing and that a high degree of privacy and concern is practiced by fellow travelers. If this factor gets in the way, you may lose the opportunity to experience some very charming little inns and guest houses, as well as historic abodes that have chosen not to alter the plumbing for the sake of architectural preservation and authenticity.

Air Conditioning: A combination of ceiling fans and air conditioning is provided in these establishments; some offer both, others just one or the other. Because the refreshing trade winds often provide ample natural ventilation, you may find that a ceiling fan is quite adequate, if not preferable. Although air conditioning sounds like a bonus, many of the units in the Caribbean are noisy and distracting and can create an unhealthy temperature fluctuation from outside to inside.

Medical Concerns: Although sophisticated medical care is available in the larger cities of the Caribbean, it is wise to travel with a medical history and ample current medications if you are under a doctor's care. The most common traveler's maladies are sunburn and sunstroke. Common sense should keep these potential problems under control, but be sure to drink plenty of liquids, wear light but protective clothing, and gradually increase exposure time in the sun.

Clothing: Packing for the Caribbean means taking light and comfortable clothing suited to the warm, tropical weather. For your stay at an intimate inn or guest house, plan for informality and very casual dress, which is in tune with the relaxed lifestyle you'll experience. For meals at nicer restaurants, plan on a casual elegance in clothing which can mean jackets for men; above all, pack as little as possible to make your trip all-around carefree. For the shared bath, take a light robe and a make-up tote for carrying the essentials "down-the-hall." Every island in the Caribbean agrees that beach attire should not be worn in town or on city streets. You will see it done, but out of respect for the local people's feelings take along and wear appropriate beach cover-ups.

Children: Traveling in the Caribbean with children can be very easy and enjoyable. Do take the following into consideration, however, to assure that your trip goes smoothly.

1. Accommodations: If you have a small child, request a room, if

possible, on the first floor. Not only are terraces and balconies potential hazards, but it can be tiresome carrying your child and all his/her paraphernalia up and down stairs (many Caribbean inns and resorts have two- and three-story buildings without elevators).

2. Food: If your child has any special dietary requirements, let your inn know in advance. It's also a good idea to bring your own baby formula, which is not always readily available on many islands. Breastfeeding moms should check if the hotel can supply distilled water. Also, don't assume that you'll be served pasteurized milk; often, you can only find raw, unpasteurized milk in the Caribbean. Ask, before you go. If it's not available, pack a supply of the airtight fresh milk cartons that don't require refrigeration or powdered milk to mix with distilled water.

3. First Aid: Though you're never too far away from medical help and assistance in the islands, it's important to pack a complete first-aid kit, especially when traveling with children. Be sure to take bandages, gauze pads and tape, scissors, antiseptic creams, antihistamines, insect repellent, calamine lotion, sun bock, and sunscreen (bring PABA-free lotions for infants). Test the sun block on your child before the trip, just in case he/she has a bad reaction. Before you go, ask your pediatrician about allergies (bee stings, flowers, shellfish) and accidents (a coral reef cut) that you might encounter—and what to do. Always carry your pediatrician's phone number.

A Word About Haiti

Due to political unrest in Haiti during the researching of this book, the author was unable to travel there. For updates on the status of tourism to the island, contact the Caribbean Tourist Organization, 20 East 46th Street, New York, New York 10017; (212) 682–0435.

Part Two

The Caribbean Inn Directory

Miami

The
Bahamas

Cuba

Cayman Islands

Jamaica

CARIBBEAN S

N

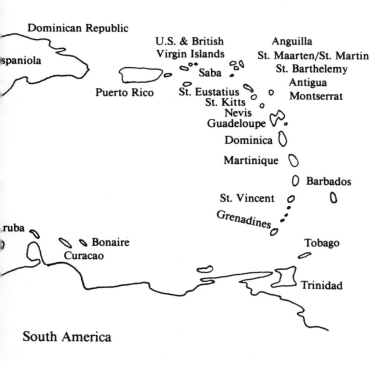

ATLANTIC OCEAN

Turks and Caicos

Dominican Republic

spaniola

U.S. & British
Virgin Islands

Anguilla

St. Maarten/St. Martin

Saba

St. Barthelemy

Antigua

Puerto Rico

St. Eustatius

St. Kitts

Montserrat

Nevis

Guadeloupe

Dominica

Martinique

Barbados

St. Vincent

Grenadines

ruba

Bonaire

Curacao

Tobago

Trinidad

South America

How To Use The Caribbean Inn Directory

Island Groupings

Recommended Island Inns: The Caribbean is divided into basic island groups with descriptions of the islands contained in each grouping. These descriptions will give you an overview of each island and help you select the type of Caribbean vacation you have in mind. Such information as the island's geography, points of interest, history, culture, currency, languages, and other practical hints will be included there.

Individual Listings

Each inn or guest house listing in the Directory is followed by an address and a phone number. A representative is included if appropriate.

Key

The *Key* information is designed to give you the opportunity to select or omit a particular spot based upon the following facts:

Type of Establishment

1. Inn—Inn or small hotel
2. Historic Inn—Inn with historical significance or restored vintage
3. Guest House—A West Indian term that can mean a private residence with guest quarters or a small hotel
4. Plantation—A former or present plantation

Number of Guestrooms

This is the total number of units available and may include cottages as well as suites.

Rates

Rates are based upon double occupancy in the following fashion: on season/off season. These rates are exclusive of room tax as well as service tax, which is common in the Caribbean. Also, be warned that rates are constantly changing and current rates should be obtained from any particular establishment before a reservation is secured. Be aware that one or more meals may be included in the rate (see "Meals" below) which could make an establishment classified as "expensive" comparably priced with one that is "moderate" but includes no meals, etc. The rate categories are broken down in the following manner:

1. Inexpensive—Less than $100
2. Moderate—$100–$150
3. Expensive—$150–200
4. Deluxe—$200 and up

Meals

Whether or not meals are included in the rates is indicated by the following:

1. EP—European Plan or without meals included.
2. CP—Continental Plan or with breakfast included.
3. MAP—Modified American Plan or breakfast and dinner included.
4. AP—American Plan or all meals included.
5. ALL—Stands for all-inclusive. This generally means that everything—all meals, airport transfers, government taxes, and entertainment—are included in the price.

Credit Cards

Indicates what credit cards are accepted, if any: American Express (AE); MasterCard (MC); VISA (VI); Diners Club (DC); Discover (DS). If all major credit cards accepted, it says credit cards accepted.

Children

Most inns and hotels throughout the Caribbean welcome children. Some, however, really pride themselves on being child-friendly. They may have special family rates and offer children's programs, children's menus, cribs, and other provisions. Whether children are welcome at any particular inn is stated in that inn's entry. If you're interested in staying at an inn, but children aren't mentioned in the entry, don't just arrive with munchkins in tow—ask when making reservations.

Smoking

Most of the establishments in this guide do allow smoking in general, but a few have limitations or do not allow smoking at all.

Location

Will give you an indication of where the inn or guest house is located.

Description

The remainder of the write-up will give you an idea of the establishment's special character: its architecture, history, furnishings, recreational offerings, location, facilities, food, grounds, entertainment, and perhaps a glimpse at its hospitable innkeepers. While some descriptions are longer than others, this does not necessarily mean that your stay will be correspondingly more or less memorable. It simply means that more information was available for some listings than for others. The "Also on the Island" listings at the end of each section include those establishments that I was unable to research thoroughly but seem worthy of inclusion and/or those establishments that provide alternative accommodations to an island's offerings, i.e., a resort listing on an island that mainly offers historic inns. *Recommended Island Inns: The Caribbean* strives to be a comprehensive guide to inns and guest houses in the Caribbean and suggests that you use the information provided as a basic guideline. It is highly recommended that you personally contact each establishment (or its agent) you are considering for more detailed information to help in your ultimate selection.

Whether your Caribbean dream vacation involves a sixteenth-century plantation, a family-run residence, or a palatial governor's mansion with gourmet cuisine, you are sure to experience a unique stay underscored with hospitality and comfort.

Turks and Caicos Islands

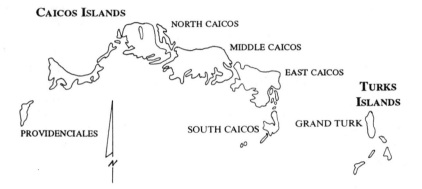

CAICOS ISLANDS

NORTH CAICOS

MIDDLE CAICOS

EAST CAICOS

TURKS
ISLANDS

PROVIDENCIALES

SOUTH CAICOS

GRAND TURK

N

*T*his little-known archipelago of islands is actually very well known to scuba divers and those who "collect" beautiful beaches. It consists of eight main inhabited islands and more than forty small cays (islets formed chiefly of coral or sand) within a 166-square-mile area and is surrounded by a continuous coral reef. Situated halfway between Miami and Puerto Rico, these protected and private islands are home to about 12,350 residents, including Turks and Caicos islanders, British, Americans, Canadians, and Haitians. English is the principal language, but many islanders also speak Creole.

Arawak Indians may have first inhabited these islands. Their discovery by Europeans is generally attributed to Ponce de Leon in 1512, although Columbus may have landed on East Caicos around 1492. Today, Turks and Caicos stands as one of the few remaining Crown Colonies, headed by a Governor appointed by Queen Elizabeth II.

Known best for its 230 miles of pure white and amber beaches as well as clear, uncrowded waters, Turks and Caicos offers an array of water sports and private, sandy retreats. The reef-surrounded islands and their calm, unpolluted waters offer skin diving, scuba, sailing, and excellent fishing.

Sightseeing expeditions will lead the visitor through rare tropical bird sanctuaries, national parks, and plantation and mining ruins. The nights here come alive with small, informal gatherings rather than nightclub life—soft calypso sounds and intimate inns and restaurants serving fresh foods from the sea.

Continuous trade-wind breezes and constant sunshine make Turks and Caicos a year-round vacation destination with temperatures averaging 77 to 83 degrees. Dress is informal and light, although protection from the tropic sun is suggested, as well as a light wrap for breezy evenings. The electrical current is compatible with North American appliances.

Getting to the islands is easy from the United States with many regular, direct flights, as well as a local airline, Cayman Airways, that departs regularly from Miami to Turks and Caicos. Turks and Caicos National Airlines provides convenient island-hopping service after your arrival. Taxis are available at most of the airports, but car rentals are handled by local businesses only. If you do drive here, remember to drive on the left side of the road.

A passport, birth certificate, or voter registration card is an acceptable form of identification; a nominal departure tax is payable upon leaving the islands. The U.S. dollar is legal tender, and full international banking is available in the major towns. Credit card use is sparse in Turks and Caicos, but the visitor will find traveler's checks welcome almost everywhere.

For more detailed information on Turks and Caicos contact:

Turks and Caicos Tourist Board
c/o The Keating Group
425 Madison Avenue
New York, NY 10017
(212) 888–4110
(800) 441–4419

✻

Meridian Club
Pine Cay, Turks and Caicos

Phone: (212) 696–4566; (800) 225–4255
Representative: Resorts Management, Inc.
Key: Inn; 13 rooms; Deluxe/Deluxe AP; AE.
Location: Between Providenciales and North Caicos.

Poised on its own 800-acre island, the Meridian Club is off in a private little world of its own. To reach it, one must fly on a small charter plane (Pine Cay has its own small airstrip) or have the club send a boat over from nearby Providenciales. The Meridian prides itself on what it doesn't have, rather than what it has. For example, there are no newspapers, no televisions, no radios, no clocks, no air conditioner, no door keys, and no telephones—anywhere.

To get around the island—which doesn't have paved roads—there are electric golf carts and bicycles. Daytime diversions include snorkeling, boating excursions to nearby cays, bird-watching, windsurfing, tennis (one court), hiking, or just sopping up the sun on the club's gaspingly beautiful 2½ mile-long beach or around its freshwater pool.

There are just thirteen rooms, strung along the beach. Each one is simple, yet elegant, with tile floors, Haitian paintings, and ceiling fan and trade wind cooling systems. All have screened-in porches, a separate dressing room, and a sitting area. There are also a dozen or

Meridian Club, Turks and Caicos Islands

so homeowner cottages on the island, some of which are available through a rental pool.

Breakfast and lunch are usually enjoyed poolside, while dinners tend to be more formal in an open-air dining room. The menu always includes a local catch such as grilled lobster, conch fritters, or grouper.

❋

Salt Raker Inn
P.O. Box 1, Grand Turk, Turks and Caicos

Phone: (809) 946–2260
Key: Historic inn; 12 units; Deluxe; EP year-round; AE, VI, MC, DS.
Location: On beach; Near town; ½ mi. to airport.

Jenny Smith has owned and managed this former shipwright's home built in the 1800s for the last three years. For many years, it was run by a couple who created a haven for guests who wanted historical ambience, very personal service, and modern conveniences. Jenny has very successfully kept the inn's traditions in place and continues to welcome back international guests year after year.

The home itself, surrounded by trees and gardens, was built by a

Bermudian family and features Bermuda-style architecture. It is in a prime location twenty-five steps from the beach and a pleasant stroll from town. The house (which is somewhere between 140 and 160 years old) contains the indoor dining room, the kitchen, the cozy guest library with lots of books and comfortable seating, and three spacious guestrooms. The recently renovated interior features Haitian paintings and carvings, and other original paintings on the walls.

The guest accommodations include rooms and suites. The suites feature living rooms, refrigerators, and large screened verandas. All of the guestrooms, located in the house and near the house, offer private baths and comfortable furnishings, attractive bedspreads and draperies, and Haitian artwork. All accommodations boast wall-to-wall carpeting, some offer air conditioners and wet-bars, and each one has a homey feel.

The outdoor dining area, decorated with beachcombing mementos and floats, is surrounded by the inn's garden filled with bougainvillea, hibiscus, and flame trees. The inn serves all three meals, and the adjacent bar provides beachside drinks, including an impressive selection of German and U.S. beers. Like the inn itself, the food is homestyle with all homemade breads, simple but good food, and plenty on the table. Dinners feature freshly caught seafood.

The usually crystal-clear sea water is just steps away from the inn and provides current-free safe swimming. Five-hundred yards from the shore is the "Wall of Turk," where divers delight in viewing

Salt Raker Inn, Turks and Caicos Islands

sponges, corals, and wildlife to a depth of 5,000 feet. The Salt Raker, like many of the resorts in this area, offers special diver packages.

✹

Also on the Islands

Kittina Hotel
Grand Turk, Turks and Caicos

Phone: (809) 946–2232; (800) KITTINA

Though not a large hotel compared to others in the Caribbean, the Kittina—with forty-eight rooms—is the largest resort on Grand Turk. It's also one of the island's liveliest and friendliest properties and is within walking distance of town. Owners Kit and Tina Fenimore opened the property about twenty years ago and have attracted a diverse clientele, ranging from divers to business people. Guests can stay in rooms with garden courtyard views or on the beach in suites with kitchenettes. Rates vary accordingly, but run from inexpensive to moderate for EP; AP and MAP supplements are available. The hotel's restaurant—which is popular among the locals—serves seafood and Continental cuisine. A full-service diving operation, Omega Divers, is on the property.

Turks Head Inn
Grand Turk, Turks and Caicos

Phone: (809) 946–2466

This one-time governor's mansion was built by a Bermudian shipwright in the late 1860s. The two-story home with gingerbread-adorned verandas has an old-fashioned garden with graceful trees and pleasant terrace. The finely constructed home sits on more than 200 feet of ocean frontage and offers a thatched patio bar and popular restaurant. The homey guestrooms are pleasant, and a few feature carved four-poster beds with canopies. The inn offers six guestrooms and rents the Drift Wood cottage next door as well. Rates are moderate year-round.

Cayman Islands

LITTLE CAYMAN

CAYMAN BRAC

GRAND CAYMAN

George
Town

N

Well to the west of the Caribbean's main archipelago (and south of Cuba), this trio of sun-bleached islands boasts some of the world's greatest diving waters. Add snorkeling, windsurfing, fishing, boating, even submarining, and you'll understand the allure of the Cayman Islands.

Formed of calcareous rock, the three islands—Grand Cayman, Little Cayman, and Cayman Brac—are quite flat in contrast to many other islands of the Caribbean that tend to be mountainous or volcanic. Grand Cayman is the largest of the islands, measuring seven by twenty-eight miles.

The islands were discovered by chance in 1503 by Christopher Columbus during his fourth voyage into the West Indies. Eighteenth-century pirate activities are legendary in these islands; "Pirates Week," a colorful festival held in late October, commemorates this swashbuckling history. The early settlers in the Cayman Islands "farmed" turtles; hence the national symbol of these islands combines the two points of history with a peg leg "turtle-pirate."

Over half of the 23,000 population is of mixed origin and the language, although basically English, is a mixture as well. An American Southern drawl is combined with the English slur and a Scottish lilt, and "v's" are pronounced as "w's" in this interesting dialect. The Cayman Islands dollar is the legal tender.

Daily scheduled flights from the United States into Grand Cayman are available, with Cayman Airways providing inter-island air service. Proof of citizenship in the form of passport, birth certificate, or voter registration is adequate, and a nominal departure tax is collected upon leaving the islands. Taxis with government-regulated rates, as well as scheduled bus service and rental cars, are available on the islands. Remember to drive on the left side of the road.

Summer or winter temperatures vary between 75 and 80 degrees in the Cayman Islands; light, casual, and comfortable clothing is appropriate everywhere. North American electrical current enables you to use your small appliances, such as dryers. The Cayman Islands are on Eastern Standard Time all year, so that during Daylight Saving Time in the Eastern U.S. the island will be one hour earlier than Eastern Daylight Time.

Each Cayman is quite different, so consider carefully how to divide your time. Grand Cayman, the hub, has been dubbed "The Switzerland of the Caribbean" because of its banking industry in George Town. It also has the most hotels and restaurants of the three islands. Cayman Brac is about as far from commercial as the sun is from the moon. You'll even see goats grazing alongside the airport runway. And then there's Little Cayman, an even more remote land that makes Gilligan's Island look over-populated.

Interested visitors can check out a giant turtle farm and a hamlet called Hell on Grand Cayman, Cayman Brac's limestone bluffs that are honeycombed with former pirate treasure caverns, or Little Cayman's migratory bird sanctuary. But the endless sugar-colored beaches and the clear, coral- and fish-filled sea complete with underwater shipwrecks are the main tourist attractions on these islands. Divers here delight in the brilliantly painted reefs and the up to 200-foot visibility, as well as the famous 1798 "Wreck of Ten Sails" at Gun Bay in Grand Cayman.

The nightlife of the islands is restricted to small clubs and intimate pubs and restaurants where food specialties include turtle steaks and turtle soup, of course.

For more detailed information on the Cayman Islands, contact:

Cayman Islands Department of Tourism
420 Lexington Ave., Suite 2733
New York, NY 10170
(212) 682–5582
or
3440 Wilshire Blvd., Suite 1202
Los Angeles, CA 90010
(213) 738–1968

✳

Eldemire's Guest House
P.O. Box 482, Grand Cayman, Cayman Islands, British West Indies

Phone: (809) 949–5387
Key: Guest house; 10 units; Inexpensive/Inexpensive EP; VI, MC.
Location: ½ mi. to beach; 1 mi. to town; 3 mi. to airport.

This charming little guest house with nine guestrooms and one furnished apartment is owned and operated by Mrs. Erma Eldemire, the hospitable former owner of Casa Bertmar (now Coconut Harbour).

27

Mrs. Eldemire and her late husband Wellesley helped to build the popular diving resort's reputation for friendliness, and Erma continues the tradition these days at her own little guest house just across the street.

The guest house is within walking distance of excellent dive sites and a short way from Seven Mile Beach. The Cove, a sugar-white beach with crystal-clear water, is just a stroll from the guest house.

Erma's casual and homey guest house has a pleasant guest lounge with fresh plants and rattan seating, but offers no restaurant. However, with some advance notice guests may have breakfast in the morning for an additional charge. Several restaurants are about half a mile away.

The four guestrooms have ceiling-fan cooling and pleasant but simple accommodations, along with private bathrooms. The one bedroom apartment can sleep six and boasts a fully-equipped kitchen.

※

Pan-Cayman House
P.O. Box 440, Grand Cayman, Cayman Islands, British West Indies

Phone: (809) 947–4002
Key: Inn; 10 units; Deluxe/Moderate-Expensive EP; No credit cards.
Location: On beach; Near town; 4 mi. to airport.

Looking more like a gracious, Georgian-style private villa, the Pan-Cayman House is actually an intimate complex of ten apartments. The white, two-story building enveloped on three sides by trees was recently refurbished; it offers two and three bedroom accommodations complete with air conditioning, a spacious living room/dining room, fully-equipped kitchen with breakfast bar, full baths, telephone, daily maid service, and private sundecks or patios with unrestricted views of beautiful Seven-Mile Beach and the Caribbean Sea of few yards ahead. Furnishings are simple but comfortable.

Along with about twenty years of hospitality, the Pan-Cayman also boasts privacy on its 200 feet of sugar-white beach, yet it lies in handy proximity to beach activity offerings along the Seven-Mile stretch. The protected leeward beach here offers wonderful swimming, snorkeling, and sailing opportunities and is particularly safe for children.

The Pan-Cayman serves no meals because each apartment has its own cooking facilities, but restaurants and entertainment are nearby. Manager Robin McCarter is on hand to see to your needs in this private retreat along the sand.

※

Coconut Harbour
P.O. Box 2086, Grand Cayman, Cayman Islands, British West Indies

Phone: (809) 949–2514; (800) 552–6281
Key: Guest house; 22 units; Expensive/Moderate EP; AE, MC, VI.
Location: 200 yds. to beach; 1 mi. to town; 2 mi. to airport.

This extended guest house is on the site of the former Casa Bertmar and, although now under new ownership, is still a small, friendly spot frequented by the diving crowd. The hotel, a few yards from the sea, has a good following that seeks its informality, camaraderie, and proximity to excellent diving sites. Waldo's Reef, which is known for its population of tame marine life, is right across the street.

Guestrooms located in a long, wooden structure are very basic, but do boast air conditioning and kitchenettes. The Bar Grill serves breakfast and lunch.

The congenial spot offers an aquasport center, short boat trips, a lively bar, and special "dive" packages for aficionados.

Jamaica

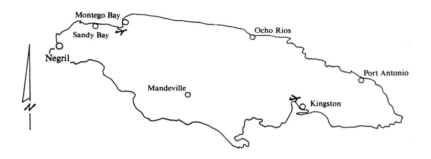

One week in Jamaica and you'll just scratch the surface. Not only is this island-nation big (the third largest of the Caribbean islands), but it's a patchwork of terrains. Jamaica's 4,400 square miles consist of lush green scenery, sugar-white beaches met by clear blue water, and a 7,400-foot mountain ridge. The 2.5 million inhabitants are mainly of African or Afro-European descent; the country's motto, "Out of Many, One People," refers to the island's many ancestors from China, India, Britain, Spain, Portugal, Germany, and the Middle East.

Formerly a Crown Colony of Great Britain, Jamaica has been an independent country since 1962, with a government similar to that of Great Britain. Jamaica's official language is the Queen's English, but Jamaicans have adopted their own variations influenced by the many nationalities there as well as the days of slavery on the island. The Jamaican dollar (J$) must be used while in the country and cannot be taken in or out of Jamaica. The rate of exchange fluctuates constantly, so check for current rates. Currency receipts for all money exchanged must be presented when leaving the country. Most major credit cards are accepted in Jamaica, and most lodging establishments use standard American electrical voltage. A converter can be requested at most that do not. Jamaican time is equal to eastern U.S. time all year. When the East practices Daylight Saving Time, Jamaica does as well.

The visitor enters Jamaica from one of two international airports, most commonly at Montego Bay. U.S. citizens are required to have proof of citizenship and ongoing or return tickets for entry and when leaving to pay a nominal departure tax. On the island there are many choices for getting around. Taxis, called *contract carriages,* have predetermined rates from area to area. However, be sure to confirm the fare beforehand and check whether they're quoting in American or Jamaican dollars. Your best bet is to keep your eyes out for the JUTA stickers on the doors of taxi cabs. These indicate they are part of the island's most reliable transportation association. Also, limousines, air-conditioned coaches, and local buses connect towns. Kingston and Montego are linked by a train, the Jamaica Railway Service, which departs twice daily on an interesting 4½-hour excursion. Rental cars and mopeds are plentiful, but remember to drive on the left. For speed, Jamaica offers an intra-island airplane service that connects the major resort areas. For getting around the Kingston and Montego Bay areas, there are buses, which are convenient and cheap.

Soft, balmy tropical breezes combine with year-round warm temperatures in Jamaica. Winter averages high-70 degree to mid-80 degree temperatures; summer goes up to 90 degrees with cooler temperatures in the Blue Mountains. Some brief daily showers are common between

October and early November, and May through early June.

Should you want to really experience Jamaican life, the Tourist Board offers a program called "Meet the People" that has operated since the sixties. The program introduces the visitor to local residents with similar interests or hobbies, often resulting in an invitation to their homes.

Kingston, with a population of 700,000, is the capital of Jamaica and the center of culture, industry, finance, and government. As the most cosmopolitan city in the country, it contains a mixture of old and new structures, with excellent dining and nightlife until dawn. Visitors here might explore the Devon House, a nineteenth-century mansion housing Jamaican crafts; Spanish Town, a colorful square surrounded by Georgian architecture; Port Royal, the former headquarters of Captain Morgan and his buccaneers; and the Hope Botanical Garden, famous for its orchid collection and Sunday afternoon band concerts.

Montego Bay, Jamaica's second largest city, dates back to 1494. Here the visitor will see great houses and plantations of the past or swim in the crystal-clear, mineral spring-fed water of Doctor's Cave Beach. An evening torch-lit canoe ride goes up the Great River, and a train ride goes through thick mountain forests to the Ipswich Coves with their eerie underworld limestone formations.

Ocho Rios was once a sleepy fishing village, but today is full of modern resorts. Open jitneys take visitors on tours to working plantations of banana, sugar cane, coconut, and breadfruit. Runaway Caves is reached by a boat ride that goes 120 feet below the earth, and a climb up Dunn's River Falls leads to cool pools. The visitor here will find Noel Coward's former home as well as Harmony Hall, a gingerbread-decked Victorian filled with up-and-coming artists' works.

Port Antonio, whose twin harbors welcome cruise ships, offers rafting expeditions, cascading falls, an ultramarine blue lagoon, and caves and caverns.

Negril has seven miles of white beach with crystalline water and all the activities that go with it. Mandeville and the south coast of Jamaica provide cool tropical mountains with spas, horseback riding, golf, bird sanctuaries, fascinating great houses, and a true Lover's Leap.

For additional information on Jamaica contact:

Jamaica Tourist Board   *or*
866 Second Avenue, 10th floor   3440 Wilshire Blvd., Ste. 1207
New York, NY 10017   Los Angeles, CA 90010
(800) 223–5224 (out of state)   (800) 421–8206 (out of state)
(212) 688–7650   (213) 384–1123

Charela Inn
P.O. Box 33, Negril Beach, Jamaica, West Indies

Phone: (809) 957–4277
Key: Inn; 39 units; Expensive–Deluxe/Expensive MAP; AE, VI, MC.
Location: On beach, 1½ mi. to town; 2 mi. to local airport.

This beachfront hacienda is located about midway along beautiful Negril Beach, hidden behind coconut palms and surrounded by gardens rich in hibiscus, orchids, and jasmine. The 1975-built inn has an elegant, Spanish villa feel with curved arches and a central fountain, yet is well equipped with all the modern amenities. Owners Daniel and Sylvie Grizzle have operated the inn for the past eleven years and, along with a cheerful staff, have earned a reputation for ultrapersonal service and delicious homemade cuisine.

A lounge with bar in the main house is available to guests and is furnished in wicker with voile draperies and marble tile floors. Guestrooms in the house and in a new wing feature both suites and bedrooms, all with full private baths, wall-to-wall carpeting, and either a balcony or a covered patio. Guest accommodations offer both air conditioning and ceiling fans and either queen size beds or two double beds. The attractively appointed guestrooms are decorated in a

Charela Inn, Jamaica

combination of tropical prints and colonial furnishings. Charela's newest suites consist of one large bedroom with queen size bed, a small bedroom with two single beds, and a full bathroom; all boast a lovely view of the sea.

A new dining room built late in 1983 has open arches with hanging flower boxes, a flower garden, a central open-air fountain, and views of the sea. The elegant setting with high-backed chairs, fine linens, and candlelight makes for romantic gourmet dinners that include five courses of French or Jamaican cuisine. A good selection of French wines is available to complement the special meals. A full English breakfast is served under umbrellas on the patio each morning, and lunches include salads, hamburgers, and house specialties.

Scuba, snorkeling, boating, and fishing are all available within walking distance of the Charela, and the staff at this friendly inn is always pleased to suggest or arrange any other activities.

❋

Hotel Astra
P.O. Box 60, 62 Ward Avenue, Mandeville, Jamaica, West Indies

Phone: (809) 962–3265
Key: Inn; 21 units; Inexpensive-Moderate EP year-round; MC, VI.
Location: 1 mi. to town; 40 mi. to beach; 70 mi. to airport.

Owner and manager Diana McIntyre-Pike gives a very personal touch to her family's home-turned-inn. The main building of the inn was a nursing home for about five years, and in 1970 the McIntyres converted it to a hotel, adding more rooms, a bar, swimming pool, and sauna. At press time, ten additional units were under construction. Diana takes pride in the family abode and its surroundings in a non-resort area just outside Mandeville, which she claims is the cleanest town in Jamaica.

The spacious grounds with interesting flowers and plants have a quiet, countryside feel. A guest lounge with red carpeting has wicker decor, and the adjoining Zodiac Room restaurant decorated in mirrors serves excellent Jamaican meals made from family recipes. Breakfast, lunch, and dinner are available to guests buffet style or with table service. A popular event is the Friday night barbecue held around the

Hotel Astra, Jamaica

pool, which provides some entertainment and attracts locals as well as visitors. Another restaurant is located near the swimming pool, and the Revival Room of the Astra serves snacks and an assortment of drinks to revive its guests, including a homemade concoction called the "Reviver," made from Guinness Stout, rum, egg, condensed milk, and nutmeg.

Each of the seventeen guestrooms and four suites at Hotel Astra is decorated individually, but all contain private baths, telephones, and radios. Guestrooms are located in the main house and in adjoining wings at this most hospitable inn.

✳

Jamaica Inn
P.O. Box 1, Ocho Rios, Jamaica, West Indies

Phone: (809) 974–2414
Representative: Caribbean World Resorts
Key: Inn; 45 units; Deluxe/Deluxe AP; AE.
Location: On the edge of town; on the beach, about 1½ hours by taxi from Montego Bay airport.

If you want to taste a little bit of Old Jamaica, this is the place to stay. The Jamaica Inn is a small, effortlessly elegant inn festooned in oleander and bougainvillea. In its earlier life, it was a private estate.

There's a main house and two wings—all painted a pale Caribbean blue. Some rooms are located right on the beach, all have air conditioning, and all are attractively furnished with chenille spreads, open-air Wedgwood-blue living areas, overstuffed sofas, and handsome writing tables. The most coveted rooms are in the ultra-private West Wing, which is literally on the water. The ultimate accommodation, which Winston Churchill stayed in back in the fifties, is the White Suite (of course you'll have to add your name to an always-long waiting list), which has its own small pool, a huge patio, and a secluded sunning bluff.

The inn is ideally situated on the most beautiful beach in Ocho Rios and offers good swimming, snorkeling, and sunfish sailing. On its spacious six-acre lawn, there's a croquet course and a freshwater pool. (Golf and tennis are available nearby.)

Dining at the Jamaica Inn is always a memorable experience, from traditional British breakfasts (with bangers and boiled tomatoes) to multi-course dinners accompanied by a small orchestra. Evenings are very formal, especially on Saturday nights in season when guests dress to the nines in black tie.

The owners of the inn—the Morrow family—are almost always on site.

✳

Native Son Villas
Manley Boulevard, Negril, Jamaica, West Indies

Phone: (809) 957–4376
Key: Cottages; 4 units; Deluxe/Expensive EP; No credit cards.
Location: On beach, 2 mi. to town; 50 mi. to airport.

If you happen to be seeking a very private holiday locale that offers plenty of activity within a short distance, Native Son Villas might be just what you're looking for. Wesley Burton, a native "son" of Jamaica who returned here from the United States to build his dream lodgings, and wife Sarah have done a beautiful job in constructing and furnishing four villas on or very near the idyllic white sand of Negril

Beach. All of the rattan and wicker furniture has been custom-constructed in Jamaica with bed mattresses, linens, and household necessities imported straight from top U.S. department stores.

All four individual villas are two-story beach houses with bedrooms and a large deck on the second floor. They feature spacious nine-foot-tall ceilings on the first floor and cathedral ceilings with exposed rafters on the second level. Villas at Native Son boast white terrazzo floors, modern kitchens, bedroom air conditioners, and ceiling fans. Guests here have a complete home and beach all to themselves with a housekeeper, caretaker, and gardener to accommodate their every need.

"Soon, Soon" Villa offers two bedrooms, each with its own bathroom. One bedroom features a king size bed and the other a double bed and twin. "Native Son" Villa has three bedrooms—one on the first floor with two twin beds, and two bedrooms on the second floor, one with a king size bed and the other offering a double and twin bed combination. The three-bedroom villa features two bathrooms, one on the first floor with shower only and a second floor bath with tub and shower. "Morning Side" and "Other Side" are Native Son's two newest villas. Completed three years ago, they each have two bedrooms.

Arriving guests at the Villas discover a bottle of Appleton Gold Rum along with a warm welcome note on the bar. The following morning the housekeeper prepares a complimentary breakfast of freshly squeezed orange juice, bacon and eggs, hard-dough bread, and Jamaican coffee to get you off to a wonderful start on your vacation. Guests buy any other food supplies, but the housekeeper will cook and serve as many meals as they wish, when they wish. Each villa boasts its own outdoor patio and brick barbecue for outside eating and relaxing.

Mornings at the beachfront, guests may buy fish or lobster caught by the local fishermen in dugout canoes. Nearby can be found all watersports, including snorkeling, scuba diving, parasailing, windsurfing, waterskiing, and boating. Jogging is a favorite on this long stretch of beach, and occasional reggae concerts are held close by.

Native Son Villas are well suited to families, couples, or groups of friends who want to have their own luxurious getaway on the beach at Negril.

✳

Richmond Hill Inn
P.O. Box 362, Union St., Montego Bay, Jamaica, West Indies

Phone: (809) 952–3859
Key: Inn; 22 units; Moderate-Expensive/Moderate-Expensive EP; Credit cards accepted.
Location: 1 mi. to beach; Near town; 3 mi. to airport.

This eighteenth-century great house was once the winter home of the Dewars of the Dewars Whiskey fame. The inn has been in operation for over twenty-eight years now, offering an informal stay in its scenic location 500 feet above the city of Montego Bay with unobstructed views of the city and bay.

Richmond Hill is perhaps better known for its restaurant, a popular tourist stop that specializes in locally caught lobster and fish. Guests find a popular bar and dining area that is covered yet open. Pretty Oriental rugs, a few antiques, and black wrought-iron tables fill the spacious eatery, which offers fine food but even better views, especially at sunset.

Adjacent to the restaurant is a picturesque swimming pool reaching out to the sea. White Grecian-type pillars and statuary and

Richmond Hill Inn, Jamaica

abundant planters and hanging potted flowers surround, as do gardens containing a small fountain.

The guestrooms at Richmond Hill are located in buildings around the grounds and are moderate but pleasant offerings. Decor features a few antiques, velveteen seating, and attractive bedspreads and drapes. Accommodations boast private baths, some television, carpeting, radio, and either balconies or patios with views of town and Montego Bay.

Live music is offered during dining hours, and the inn offers courtesy transportation to Doctor's Cave Beach and shops.

✳

Sandals Inn
P.O. Box 412, Kent Avenue, Montego Bay, Jamaica, West Indies

Phone: (809) 952–4140; (800) 726–3257
Representative: Unique Vacations
Key: Inn; 52 units; Deluxe/Deluxe (3 nights minimum) ALL; Credit cards accepted.
Location: Across from beach; 1½ mi. to town; 1 mi. to airport.

This white colonial-style hotel with picturesque sea views offers a relaxed, house-guest feel to its visitors, all of whom are couples (male and female). The three-story villa-type structure has undergone extensive remodeling over the last several years that includes new carpeting and furnishings in most of the rooms and a most attractive facelift to its common areas.

The fifty-two accommodations are arranged in an open horseshoe fashion around a very inviting central courtyard with beautiful pool, Jacuzzi, and outdoor dining—all in a privately gated tropical setting. The guestrooms range from deluxe offerings with choice views of the sea from the veranda, to standard accommodations with a garden view. For the modest difference in price, the seaview accommodations are definitely the ones to request—if you can find one available! All of the rooms feature individual air conditioning, private tiled bathrooms, built-in hair dryers, and telephones. The upgraded units boast green carpeting with attractively coordinated bedspreads; deluxe rooms all offer radios and king-size beds.

The lobby of Sandals Inn is quite spacious and elegant with

Sandals Inn, Jamaica

friendly porters and management ready to serve. A tour desk is staffed day and night here to help with any special tours the guest would like to arrange. Wool-carpeted stairs with brass holders lead up from the center of the marbled lobby to the two floors above that are the guestrooms of the hotel.

Overlooking the pool courtyard is the great house-designed restaurant of the inn with white arches, peppermint green and pastel shade interiors, chandeliers, candlelight, and Jamaican fretwork. Lots of tropical foliage is draped around the bay window alcove seating and semi-circular banquettes. Guests may take breakfast, lunch, and dinner here or in the delightful attached courtyard, as well as enjoy drinks at the bar. An excellent parquet floor for dancing and more intimate seating are offered there as well. The restaurant features specialty nights such as the "Surf and Turf Night," with a lobster and steak buffet and live piano music, and the "Seafood Night" with fresh local catch in a five-course menu and live calypso entertainment. The award-winning meals at the hotel are priced within reason, and note that the delicious breakfasts are included in stays of seven days or more.

A guest lounge sits opposite the restaurant on the other side of the pool/courtyard. Its newly redecorated interiors feature pretty French doors, colonial and antique decor, a small library, a card table, and satellite television. The comfortable area is decorated in green and pink prints with warm wallcoverings and plump sofas and chairs.

Sandals Inn is a short walk from well-known Doctor's Cave Beach and Cornwall Beach, with their accompanying watersports offerings, and is also within walking distance of many small shops and businesses. Not surprisingly, many guests at the hotel choose to spend a lot of time in the inviting courtyard/pool area, sipping Jamaican specialties and nibbling at fresh tropical fruit. Your gracious host at Sandals Inn is John Terry.

✳

Terra Nova Hotel
17 Waterloo Road, Kingston 10, Jamaica, West Indies

Phone: (809) 926–2211
Key: Inn; 35 units; Moderate EP year-round; Credit cards accepted.
Location: Near town; 14 mi. to beach; 17 mi. to airport.

This white colonial mansion with broad arches, graceful balustrades, and romantic night-time lighting sits in a quiet, secluded residential section close to town. The mansion was built as an elegant residence in 1921 and converted to a small hotel in 1959. In October of 1984 the entire inn on five acres of well-manicured grounds was refurbished and stands as one of the most intimate and charming small hostelries on the island.

Terra Nova offers guests an attractive lounge with carefully selected period furnishings and a crystal chandelier. Several meeting rooms with similar decor are available for private groups, making the hotel a popular choice for business travelers who enjoy hotel-type services in more intimate surroundings. The El Dorado dining room of the inn boasts attractive deep coral walls, Hepplewhite chairs, mahogany tables set in fine linens, and arched windows overlooking the garden. Both lunches and dinners are served in these elegant surroundings. Breakfast is served on the outside terrace with lovely views of town, greenery, and the mountains. The inn offers light flute and guitar music twice weekly.

The guestrooms at Terra Nova contain all the modern amenities, including central air conditioning, telephone, television, and bath. The contemporarily furnished rooms are color-coordinated in shades of gray, white, and peach, and from the balconies you can see the Blue Mountains in the distance.

Nestled behind the villa, among the shade trees, brilliant

poinsettias, and well-tended gardens, is the swimming pool. Golf, water sports, and other recreation are available nearby, and Kingston's convention center and main shopping are just a few minutes away.

❋

Tryall Golf, Tennis, and Beach Club
Sandy Bay Post Office, Hanover Parish, Jamaica, West Indies

Phone: (809) 952–5110 or 952–5111; (800) 336–4571
Representative: Robert Reid Assoc.
Key: Plantation; 52 units; Deluxe/Deluxe MAP; Credit cards accepted.
Location: On beach; 12 mi. to town; 15 mi. to airport.

The tastefully restored and decorated great house at the core of this resort was built in 1834 and stood in the heart of a rich 2,200-acre sugar plantation. The former plantation, now rich in bougainvillea, towering palms, and flowering trees, has been transformed into a gracious historic inn with full resort offerings (including possibly the best golf in the Caribbean) and a spectacular location on a sugar-white curve of beach. All of this luxury that includes lodging, breakfast, and dinner costs a bit more, but is one of the better bargains in the hotel's short off-season periods of November 1 through December 14 and April 15 through May 15. The hotel itself is closed April 30 through November 1, although other resort offerings remain open year-round.

The Tryall Great House, surrounded by immaculately manicured lawns and flowering plants, has a country manor feel on the inside created by designer color schemes, overstuffed furnishings in coordinated chintz fabrics, French doors, and small-paned windows with views of the sea and plantation countryside. This decor combines both the tropical and elegant with the use of fresh white walls, striking colors, and nice touches such as fresh flowers and potted palms.

Guests at Tryall enjoy a sitting room and lounge in the great house as well as the equally intimate and gracious dining room with beamed ceilings, tropical planters, pink and coral linens, comfortable seating, and French doors that lead to the terrace with breathtaking views of the sea. Gourmet dinners include entrees of lemon veal, lamb

Tryall Golf, Tennis, and Beach Club, Jamaica

chops with mint sauce, Jamaican seafood platter, and medallions of beef. Lunch may be enjoyed by the sea at the Beach Cafe, and a full breakfast with extensive selections is served in the dining room or al fresco on the inspiring terrace. After 6:30 P.M. gentlemen generally wear sports jackets with or without ties and ladies wear cocktail attire. Music and dancing are evening pastimes at the great house.

The fifty-two recently refurbished guestrooms of the great house are all individually decorated and air conditioned and offer various views of the dramatic scenery. All of the guest accommodations have private baths, telephone, patio or balcony, and attractively coordinated decor with an airy, tropical feel. The spacious rooms mostly offer sitting areas, fresh white walls, framed prints, and tasteful and comfortable furnishings.

For recreation there are nine Laykold courts (five with lights), an excellent diving and sailing ocean with beach, a large swimming pool with swim-up bar directly in back of the great house, and the pride of the establishment: a championship eighteen-hole, 6,800-yard golf course. In fact, Tryall uses a water wheel as its logo because of the plantation's original water wheel, which has been restored and now stands as the backdrop to the course's sixth tee. The restored 200-year-old wheel that once supplied the power for the mill now provides water for the green, flowing fairways of the golf club.

Tryall Golf and Beach Club is overseen by expert general manager Robert Raedisch.

Note: As previously mentioned, the hotel great house is closed April 30 through November 1, but the Tryall also offers luxurious villas in secluded areas around the grounds that are available year-round. These villas offer private pools and full staffs.

✳

Also on the Island

De Montevin Lodge Hotel
21 Fort George Street, P.O. Box 85, Port Antonio, Jamaica, West Indies

Phone: (809) 993–2604

This late-1800s Victorian with detailed trim is family run and offers hospitality and reasonable rates near town. The fifteen guestrooms are simply furnished but tidy and include both private bath and shared bath offerings. The budget-minded rates include breakfast. A comfortable lounge with television and a small bar is available for guests, as are a porch and side patio. Good Jamaican dinners are offered.

Seville Guest House
P.O. Box 1385, Sunset Avenue, Montego Bay, Jamaica, West Indies

Phone: (809) 952–2814 or 952–3662

This enclave of accommodations near Cornwall Beach is made up of rental villas, apartments, and a guest house. The five extremely budget-minded house offerings feature air conditioning, private bath, separate living room with television, and free airport pick-up. The furnishings are very simple, but maid service is provided, and the beach is within walking distance. No meals are served on the premises. Villas are available by the week.

Dominican Republic

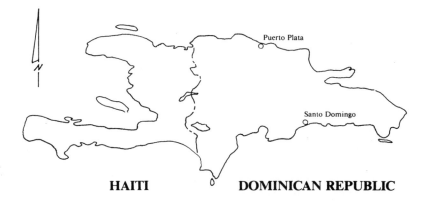

Puerto Plata

Santo Domingo

HAITI   DOMINICAN REPUBLIC

HISPANIOLA

*O*nly fifty-four miles from Puerto Rico, sharing the island of Hispaniola with Haiti, is the Dominican Republic. Situated on the eastern half of the island, this still unspoiled Caribbean nation contains the highest peak in the West Indies, Pico Duarte, with an elevation of 10,417 feet. The interior of the island is lush and produces rich sugar cane; the coastline is characterized by miles and miles of beautiful coral beaches. The Dominican Republic has the largest number of hotel rooms in the Caribbean (16,000 at last count). Since most of them are in large hotels and resorts, you will find we have recommended just one property.

The language of the Dominican Republic is Spanish, but English is becoming more common. Likewise, the peso is the currency although many establishments will accept the U.S. dollar. It is wise to have any money exchanges handled at a bank or exchange house to be sure you are receiving the proper exchange rate. United States and Canadian citizens are required to provide proof of citizenship with a passport, voter's registration card, or birth certificate, and to buy a tourist card upon entering the country. A nominal departure tax is collected in pesos upon leaving the Dominican Republic.

The Dominican Republic is on Atlantic Standard Time (one hour later than Eastern Standard Time) except during Daylight Saving season when the time on the island and in the Eastern U.S. is the same. The electrical current is compatible with U.S. appliances.

Getting around the Dominican Republic can be achieved in several ways, but it is not always easy. Taxis are available at major hotels and the airport, but are not metered. If you are able to conquer language differences, be sure to decide on cost before hiring your taxi. Taxis may also be rented for sightseeing excursions but at a much greater cost than a bus tour. Regularly scheduled buses get you around the city of Santo Domingo for very reasonable rates. Car rentals, available in Santo Domingo and Puerto Plata, are relatively inexpensive and include Budget and Hertz. Driving is on the right side of the road.

The capital of the Dominican Republic, Santo Domingo, is the oldest city in the New World, with a colonial area whose streets were trod by none other than Columbus himself. Museums that are restored examples of former palaces, sixteenth-century homes, and monasteries have been opened to the public as "living" history lessons. The Alcazar was a palace built for Columbus's son and is full of precious antiques, tapestries, and art. The National Pantheon was a 1714 Jesuit monastery as well as a warehouse for tobacco; the Museo de las Casas Reales was the Governor's residence and is decorated in colonial artifacts.

Entertainment abounds both day and night in Santo Domingo. A large park, the Plaza de la Cultura, contains the National Theater, which puts on local concerts and ballets. Horseracing, tennis, golf, and champion deep-sea fishing are available, but the nicer beaches, rated high for scuba and snorkeling, are a distance out of town. Nightlife in Santo Domingo includes many discos, gambling casinos, and Las Vegas-type acts with local talent.

Shoppers in the Dominican Republic will enjoy the handcrafted items found in the colorful market places, small shops, and more modern shopping complexes. Among the attractive bargains are various jewelry items fashioned out of the national gem, amber, and macrame and mahogany items.

Puerto Plata, meaning "port of silver," was named for the ships that stopped here full of treasures from the New World. Today it is a busy cruise ship stop and is a mixture of modern and old-world charm. Cobblestone streets and outlying sugar cane fields are mixed with industry and signs of growth.

The visitor to the Dominican Republic will also find one of the largest sugar mills in the world, coral reefs, and shipwrecks, as well as undersea gardens, a fifteenth-century artists' colony, and a secluded island off the coast for sunbathing and snorkeling.

For more detailed information contact:

Dominican Tourist Information Center
485 Madison Avenue
New York, NY 10022
(212) 826–0750

✳

Hostal Palacio Nicholas de Ovando

53 Calle las Damas, Santo Domingo, Dominican Republic

Phone: (809) 687–7181
Key: Historic inn; 55 units; Inexpensive year-round EP; AE, DC, VI, MC.
Location: In town; 20 mi. to airport.

Historic in every way, this large-scale inn is the namesake of the sixteenth-century governor of Hispaniola, is created from two lovely, restored fifteenth-century mansions, and sits in the heart of the historic district of Old Town. History lies on every side of the inn, and within the weathered walls of the hotel, there is a palace fit for a prestigious resident, in this case its many overnight guests.

The common rooms of the inn are bedecked in colonial-era antiques, ceremonial tapestries, and bronzed mirrors. The classic courtyards give views of the Ozama River and are peaceful retreats complete with bubbling fountains, umbrella-covered tables, and the original arches of the mansions. A swimming pool with pleasant sunning terrace and adjoining bar makes up for the lack of nearby beach facilities. A good restaurant, Extremadura, is a part of the hotel and serves all three meals amid its antique Spanish decor, highlighted by a high beamed ceiling and gilded chandeliers.

The guestrooms at the Nicolas de Ovando carry out the antique feel with many colonial-era reproduction beds, imported hardwood furnishings, beamed ceilings, and tile floors. The rooms are all air conditioned and boast private baths with attractive hand-painted tile. Some have views of the port, others overlook the pool or the colonial zone.

Puerto Rico

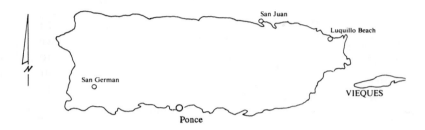

*T*he Puerto Rico Tourism Office invites the tourist to "follow the footsteps of the early Spanish conquistadores from the cobblestones of [the] historic city of San Juan to the luxurious vegetation of [the] tropical forests to the beautiful white sand beaches . . ." Add to this a bustling strip of casinos and nightlife-filled hotels, and it sums up the varied offerings of the Caribbean's number one tourist destination, Puerto Rico.

San Juan, the capital of the 100-mile-long by 35-mile-wide island, is a mixture of old and new. Historic Old San Juan's narrow streets are lined with sixteenth- and seventeenth-century buildings and lead to El Morro, a four-century-old fortress, and a central plaza surrounded by charming boutiques and sidewalk cafes. In abrupt contrast is the city's Condado strip, packed with high-rise hotel casinos, international restaurants, fast-food familiars, and night clubs with lavish spectacles and live music.

But outside of San Juan, Puerto Rico offers visitors a lush tropical rain forest, El Yunque, with orchids, waterfalls, and rare birds, a crescent-shaped, coconut tree-lined beach called Luquillo, and magical Phosphorescent Beach. Across the island is Ponce, the second largest city in Puerto Rico, where an ancient black and red firehouse now houses a tourism information office.

Getting to and from Puerto Rico is easy because it boasts the most extensive air service in the Caribbean, with daily flights from all major North American cities. No passports or visas are required for U.S. citizens, and the currency is the U.S. dollar. Major banks are located in San Juan, and credit cards are widely accepted. English is spoken extensively here as well. Puerto Rico is on Atlantic Standard Time (one hour ahead of Eastern Standard Time) but does not recognize Daylight Saving Time. Therefore, in Daylight Saving season Puerto Rico's clocks are in harmony with those in Eastern U.S. states.

Local transportation is plentiful with metered taxis, *publicos*, on frequent schedules between towns, several rental car agencies, sightseeing buses, and regularly scheduled bus service around town. *Publicos* or public cars charge per person for destination requested and are in the habit of picking up passengers along the way. It is wise to be aware that this form of transportation can be economical but at times may take longer than anticipated. An old-fashioned trolley shuttles between the public parking lots and the narrow streets of Old San Juan.

Sports on the island include all the beach and ocean offerings: snorkeling, scuba, surfing, and fishing, although some beaches are better suited in terms of clarity of water and general beauty. Tennis; horseback riding on mountain trails; a race track, El Comandante; and ten eighteen-hole golf courses make recreational opportunities pretty much unlimited.

Puerto Rico offers its own brand of personal inn; a few are mentioned in this guide. The "parador" is a simple inn found in the countryside and is government-sponsored. For general information about the paradores, call (800) 443–0266 or (809) 721–2884. Also, the out-islands of San Juan, Culebra, and Vieques provide some charming guest house accommodations.

For more detailed information on Puerto Rico contact:

Puerto Rico Tourism Company
575 Fifth Avenue
New York, NY 10017
(212) 599–6262
(800) 223–6530 (outside N.Y.)

✳

Arcade Inn
#8 Taft Street, San Juan, Puerto Rico 00911

Phone: (809) 725–0668
Key: Guest house; 19 units; Inexpensive/Inexpensive EP; VI, MC.
Location: Condado; 75 ft. to beach; 3 mi. to airport.

This hospitable inn can be found on a Condado area side-street populated by various multiple housing developments. The three-story, Spanish-style house stands out as an intimate retreat for guests just a few feet from the beach. Resident owners Aurelio and Renee Cinque have made this a popular guest house, as they personally see to guests from the moment they arrive to the time they depart. The only other staff in attendance consists of housekeeping personnel who keep the simple quarters spotless.

The white residence with olive green trim has attractive arches and scallops, and the guest enters through a neat patio area with potted plants and concrete tables and chairs on the side of the house. Arched, iron-grill doors lead to the office in this front structure and the guestrooms contained within. An annex building in the back of the property provides efficiency units and cabana-style rooms.

Guest accommodations at the guest house are all very pleasant, especially those with views of the ocean; each unit is a little different in

Arcade Inn, Puerto Rico

size and shape. The main house offers several rooms with balconies, and some of the rear units have private patios. All of the guest accommodations have cheerful curtains and bedspreads, private shower-baths with pretty tilework, and nicely waxed floors.

Adjacent to the rear structure is the patio bar that serves breakfast, sandwiches, and drinks all day in a relaxed outdoor setting. The continental breakfast of juice, coffee, toast, and jelly and the full American-style morning meal are very reasonably priced. Picnic lunches are also available if ordered in advance. Guests may keep their own supply of cold drinks or fruit in the guest refrigerator in this area.

The Cinques enjoy playing host to their many return guests, who come from all over the world. Mr. Cinque speaks five languages, which enables him to easily convey that "his home is your home."

✳

El Canario Inn
1317 Ashford Avenue, San Juan, Puerto Rico 00907

Phone: (809) 722–3861
Key: Inn; 25 units; Inexpensive/Inexpensive CP; AE, VI, MC, DC.
Location: Condado; 1 block to beach, 4 mi. to airport.

This informal inn is a small oasis of individuality nestled among the high-rises and casinos of the Condado. The 1923-built, Spanish-style structure with tile roof and heavy wrought iron was originally a doctor's residence. Several small buildings in the rear have been combined with the former residence to make up El Canario, located within a block of all the Condado action. For added convenience the city bus passes directly in front of the inn.

The guest enters the inn through a small guest lounge with color television and comfortable seating. A round-the-clock reception desk is here, manned by the friendly staff and owner-manager Keith Olson. Some of the inn's guestrooms are located on the three floors of this building. Guests will also find a small communal kitchen with guest refrigerator in this building on their way out to the attractive side patio.

The brick patio of the inn is protected from the busy Ashford Avenue noises by a tall wall and relaxed tropical vegetation. Guests at El Canario seem to gravitate to this inviting spot both day and night. In the morning a serve-yourself, complimentary breakfast is offered on the patio. A toaster flanked by various breads, butter, and jams is provided along with lots of coffee or milk. Guests help themselves and take a seat at one of the large covered patio tables for some friendly socializing in addition to the morning fare. No other meals are offered at the inn, but you are within easy walking distance of a number of good restaurants.

Just past the side patio area are convenient cold drink and ice machines and then the picturesque stone-decorated pool. This is the afternoon gathering spot for the congenial guests at El Canario as they chat, sunbathe, and swim in the small but pretty pool, with fountain, waterfall, and handy built-in drink table. The other small buildings that hold guestrooms at the inn are situated near the pool; some of those contain efficiency units. A convenient guest laundromat is also in this vicinity.

The guestrooms at El Canario are very basic and often petite. The walls are freshly painted white splashed with some local artwork, and bamboo curtains grace the windows. The asphalt tile floors are adequate, but the bright floral or geometric print bedspreads liven up the rooms. A compact, tiled shower-bath and air conditioning are found in all the guestrooms. Either director's chairs or rattan seating is provided, as well as ample closet and dresser clothes storage. The quieter accommodations are located in the rear buildings of the inn.

Although the accommodations are not luxurious at El Canario, no one seems to mind. In fact, the heavy repeat clientele at this informal inn attests to its popularity as a congenial spot where the guest can be totally involved in the fast pace of the Condado or just relax in this friendly hideaway that is also kind to the budget.

※

The Horned Dorset Primavera Hotel
Apartado 1132, Rincon, Puerto Rico 00743

Phone: (809) 823–4030
Representative: Caribbean Inns, Ltd.
Key: Inn; 24 units; Deluxe/Deluxe EP; AE, MC, VI.
Location: On the water; 15 minute drive from Mayaguez.

Beautifully situated on Puerto Rico's west coast, the Horned Dorset Primavera Hotel offers wonderful privacy and seclusion. Its twenty-four suites are housed in half a dozen two-story villas and a main house, all in Spanish-Mediterranean style. Each suite is attractively decorated with mahogany furniture (including four-poster beds) and has stucco walls and red-tile floors. Each one also has a balcony or patio that looks out to the sea. Bathrooms are luxuriously

The Horned Dorset Primavera Hotel, Puerto Rico

appointed with Italian marble and shining brass fixtures (and a bidet).

The centerpiece of the hotel is the two-story main building that has a terrace (for breakfasts and lunches), a library, and a formal dining room.

A pool, some of the country's most beautiful beaches, and the site of the world surfing championships are nearby.

*

La Condesa Inn
Calle Cacique #2071, San Juan, Puerto Rico 00911

Phone: (809) 727–3698 or 727–3900
Key: Inn; 16 units; Inexpensive/Inexpensive CP; VI, MC, AE.
Location: Ocean Park; 100 ft. to beach; 4 mi. to airport.

La Condesa Inn is hidden away on a residential street just a mile from the shops and restaurants on the Condado. The inn, composed of two 1954-built homes (one formerly a Spanish consul's residence), is locked behind a large wall. Only guests have keys to the gate for optimum privacy and security, giving it a home-like feel. The exteriors of the two structures are attractive with pretty orangish-rust awnings and balconies.

Within the walls of the inn the guest will discover instant tranquility provided by waterfalls, goldfish ponds, and planters filled with tropical plants. This patio area with covered dining and bar is the site of the complimentary morning meal served from 8 to 10 A.M. each day. Guests relax at quaint ice cream tables and chairs placed around the terra-cotta floors and enjoy the continental fare. Breakfast may be upgraded for a minimal additional charge to a full breakfast with bacon or ham, eggs, French toast, or omelettes. Lunch, with a large variety of sandwiches, is served here between noon and 3 P.M. Dinner is not presently offered, but the "Two Gates Patio Bar" stays in operation, beginning with your complimentary cocktail upon arrival.

Adjacent to the patio is a spacious swimming pool molded in a scalloped design. The privacy wall that protects sunbathers from the street serves as a scenic diversion with four mini-waterfalls cascading down the stone-embedded concrete. This touch adds to the many tranquil aspects of the inn. Serenity and privacy are also provided in the courtyard/patio layout of the guestrooms themselves. A combination of

La Condesa Inn, Puerto Rico

individual striped awnings over guestroom doors, tiny patios dotted with neat potted plants, and quiet courtyards between building areas creates a quiet, private feel.

The guestrooms at La Condesa Inn all contain private baths with tub/showers and attractive ceramic tile floors. Each guestroom is individually decorated, but each features such detailing as pretty bedspreads and shower curtains, cleverly used mirrors that enlarge the more modestly sized rooms, large closets, cheerful wallcoverings, and radios. A few of the units boast television and kitchens; most offer pleasant balconies or patios. All of the guestrooms at the inn are immaculately kept.

La Condesa Inn remains a well-kept secret in many ways. A majority of the inn's guests are repeat clientele or have been referred by word of mouth. The service, under the careful eye of owner Reynaldo Alvarez, is friendly and accommodating.

✳

El Convento
100 Calle Cristo, P.O. Box 1048, San Juan, Puerto Rico 00902

Phone: (809) 723–9020; (800) 468–2779
Key: Historic inn; 99 units; Moderate-Expensive/Moderate-Expensive
EP; AE, DC, MC, VI.
Location: Old San Juan; 3 mi. to beach; 8 mi. to airport.

El Convento, Puerto Rico

The El Convento is one of Old San Juan's proud historical land-marks. Owned by the government of Puerto Rico, the hotel, steeped in centuries of rich history, is itself a restored treasure. The original seventeenth-century convent was closed in disrepair in 1903 as a nun's retreat and reopened as a special historical inn many years later, after careful restoration that incorporated most of the original architecture, tile, and beams.

The pink stucco Spanish building with tall white columns and black iron railings is situated in the heart of the historic city, fronted by the quaint cobblestone streets of town. Guests enter through the massive wooden doors to a lobby decorated in Mediterranean-style antiques, giant wall tapestries, and black and white marble flooring. The hotel complex, surrounding an attractive courtyard area, is a melding of arches, hand-painted tiles, chandeliers, antiques, and carved wooden beams.

59

The guestrooms of the hotel number ninety-nine, disqualifying it for an "intimate inn" classification, but each guestroom has an identity of its own in keeping with the seventeenth-century Spanish heritage of the building. All guestrooms have the modern amenities of color televisions, private modern baths, radios, and air conditioning, but many are decorated in elegant four posters with canopies, velveteen seating, and various antique pieces.

Dining at the hotel is on the delightful atrium patio in the courtyard with breakfast bar or in the more formal dining hall. A small but attractive pool is located in the central courtyard as well.

The hotel offers free transportation to the Condado Beach, and entertainment is provided nightly, with flamenco shows twice a week.

✳

Parador Martorell
Ocean Drive 6-A, P.O. Box 384, Luquillo Beach, Puerto Rico 00673

Phone: (809) 889–2710; (800) 443–0266
Key: Inn; 7 units; Inexpensive/Inexpensive CP; AE, VI, MC.
Location: ¹/₂ blk. to beach; Near town; 45 min. to airport.

In business now for over twenty-five years, Parador Martorell is distinguished as the pioneer of the government parador program, Paradores Puertoriquenos. The paradores are country inns that have been set up with the encouragement of the government to foster tourism in other parts of the island to let the visitor know that Puerto Rico has a lot more to offer than San Juan itself.

This parador opened in 1966 and was designed personally by the late owner-manager Irma Martorell. Today, it is very meticulously run by her niece, Maria Teresa Martorell.

The modern two-story structure features a ground-floor patio garden/guest lounge where the complimentary breakfast buffet with local and international dishes is served during on-season. This pleasant patio is surrounded by tropical foliage, palms, and lemon and orange trees. The seven guestrooms at the inn all have shared baths, except one, and are decorated in colorful posters and paintings by local artists. Double- and twin-bedded rooms are available, as well as some with terraces or balconies.

In addition to the intimacy of the inn, one of the most appealing aspects is its location just a few minutes by car from pretty Luquillo Beach, which is just half a block away. The Parador Martorell will provide free beach towels for sunning, and scuba and snorkeling arrangements can be made. Also, the inn is very convenient to El Yunque, the rain forest, and to the ferry to the outer islands. The parador is about an hour's ride from Old San Juan and forty-five minutes from the airport. As you might guess, this stop is most convenient when you're renting a car, or you might opt to spend all your time at the parador, which is within easy walking distance of town or the beach.

❋

The Parador Oasis
Calle Luna #64, P.O. Box 144, San German, Puerto Rico 00753

Phone: (809) 892–1175; (800) 443–0266
Key: Historic Inn/Inn; 52 units; Inexpensive EP year-round; VI, MC, AE, DC.
Location: 20 mi. to beach; 1 mi. to town; 18 mi. to airport (Mayaguez).

One of a handful of island paradores or country inns, the Oasis is a sublime historical addition located in the oldest community of Puerto Rico, San German. The small town of San German retains its Spanish-colonial charm with two picturesque plazas—the beautiful Porta Coeli Church (a 1606 monastery) with eighteenth-century art, and the eighteenth-century Parador Oasis, which was originally a family mansion, later a winery, and for many years a hostelry.

The Spanish-colonial style mansion with decorative latticework and ornate verandas offers a total of fifty-two guestrooms, all with new furnishings, air conditioning, and color television. About half of them overlook the pool; the others surround a lush courtyard.

The Parador has a pool, a Jacuzzi, a sauna, and a gym. Its old carriage house has been restored and converted to a contemporary disco, "The Club Elite," that holds up to 400 and serves as a multi-purpose room for seminars, weddings, banquets, and parties overlooking the romantic courtyard of the inn. The lobby of the inn is located in the old living room of the mansion and is marked by impressive eighteenth-century frescos uncovered during restoration. The restaurant is located in the arcade surrounded by graceful arches and brickwork with views of the pool and poolside dining tables.

An a la carte menu is available Monday through Thursday with "Special of the Day" lunches featuring Puerto Rican and continental dishes. Friday night starts with happy hour and live music, followed by a buffet with local fish delicacies. Saturday's offerings include a rum cocktail party poolside, buffet, fashion show, and dancing. Sunday's schedule is more relaxing with a late buffet, aerobics if you like, and live poolside music from noon to 4:00 P.M. Note that the inn also allows a late check-out time of 4:00 P.M. on Sundays so that guests may move as slowly as they wish.

Many tours and activities are arranged for guests, and the Oasis is a mere five-minute walk from fourteen historical landmarks in the quaint town. Safe beaches are about twenty-five minutes away by car or the inn can arrange transportation for a small charge.

❋

Tres Palmas
2212 Park Boulevard, San Juan, Puerto Rico 00913

Phone: (809) 727–4617 or 727–5434
Key: Guest house; 10 units; Moderate/Inexpensive CP; MC, VI, AE.
Location: 1 mi. to Condado; Across from beach; 2 mi. to airport.

This impeccably neat, gray Spanish-style house with tile roof is locked behind a wrought-iron gate. The petite hacienda beckons a small group of guests who delight in its intimacy as well as its outstanding unobstructed views of the Atlantic just across the roadway. Within the gates is an attractive gravel garden with potted tropical specimens and a small pond with bridge. The front porch area, a popular lounging and breakfasting spot for guests, looks over this tidy little front garden to the ocean activity just beyond.

Tres Palmas received a new owner, Elvin Torres, who brought about a great deal of remodeling to the grounds and guestrooms. The pleasant and modest guest accommodations boast little touches such as attractive wallcoverings, mirrors over the beds, and modern, private baths (except two rooms that share one bath), making the stay here a good value. All of the guestrooms at the bed and breakfast boast air conditioning, clock radios, and separate outside entrances. A few of the

Tres Palmas, Puerto Rico

guestrooms offer color cable television as well. There are also two efficiency apartments in a neighboring building.

Guests at Tres Palmas enjoy a complimentary continental breakfast daily and a refreshing "welcome" pina colada. Tres Palmas's helpful manager is Glen Sullivan.

Lounging at Tres Palmas is encouraged in every way. A small "mini-pool" that looks more like a Jacuzzi has been fitted into the only pool space available on the property. It is intimate, but relaxing nonetheless. Hidden on the roof of the house, at the top of rather steep spiral stairs, is a spacious sundeck with a spectacular view over the palms of the Atlantic's horizon. This attractive escape is furnished with umbrella tables, shaded lounges, and lounges open completely to the sun. Potted plants and cactus add a pretty touch, but can't compete with the views. This is an ideal, protected spot to sun when the wind begins to blow.

✳

Vieques Island (Out Island)

La Casa del Francés
P.O. Box 458, Vieques Island, Puerto Rico 00765

Phone: (809) 741–3751
Key: Historic inn; 18 units; Moderate MAP/Inexpensive EP; AE, MC, VI.
Location: 7 min. walk to beach; Countryside; 5 mi. to airport.

La Casa del Francés, Puerto Rico

The island of Vieques, a part of Puerto Rico, can be reached via a ferry boat ride from Fajardo or by small aircraft from the Isla Grande Airport. The air trip will be much more comfortable for those who are troubled by a fairly frisky sea crossing. Vieques, like this charming parador, offers uncrowded tropical countryside and long stretches of white sand lined with palms. Though it takes a little bit of effort to get there, La Casa del Francés offers those seeking a quiet getaway a bit of history mixed with personal attention.

La Casa del Francés is a turn-of-the-century plantation house and has been designated an historical landmark by the government of Puerto Rico. La Casa, situated on a knoll top, boasts beautiful architecture of the era, marked by seventeen-foot-high ceilings and wide verandas. The guestrooms tend to be spacious with the same high ceilings, simple but cheerful decor, shutters, old-fashioned fans, and French doors; all feature private baths. Guest accommodations in the mansion surround an airy two-story atrium.

The outdoor dining room at the inn has a lovely view of the tropical grounds and the inviting swimming pool. All three meals are offered here at reasonable prices.

Sun Bay Beach, a popular, palm-fringed stretch, is within walking distance of the inn; the tiny fishing village of Esperanza is also a short walk away. Arrangements can be made there for fishing trips, night cruises on Phosphorescent Bay (an inspiring phenomenon), and snorkeling or scuba.

U.S. Virgin Islands

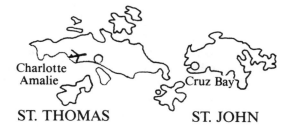

Charlotte
Amalie

Cruz Bay

ST. THOMAS

ST. JOHN

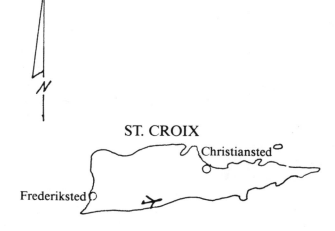

N

ST. CROIX

Christiansted

Frederiksted

*I*n all there are some fifty islands that make up the U.S. Virgin Islands, some no bigger than rock formations protruding from the incredibly clear aqua sea. The main islands are St. Croix, the largest, St. John, and St. Thomas, the latter two just thirty-five miles from St. Croix and three miles apart from each other. These islands, lying between the Atlantic Ocean and the Caribbean Sea, were discovered in 1493 by Columbus, who named them the "Virgins" due to their unspoiled beauty. A history that includes almost 200 years of Danish rule and a rich, pirate-inviting trade has left intriguing marks on these islands for the visitor to discover.

In 1917 the United States purchased these islands and, as they form a U.S. unincorporated Territory, all residents born here are U.S. citizens. Visitors are not required to have passports, but identification such as a voter's registration card or birth certificate is required. The language spoken is English and the currency is, of course, the U.S. dollar. Traveler's checks and credit cards are honored in these islands extensively, but not personal checks. The U.S. Virgin Islands is on Atlantic Standard Time (one hour ahead of Eastern Standard Time) except during Daylight Saving Time when U.S. Virgin Island time and Eastern Daylight Time are the same.

Another benefit of being a part of the United States is shopping in the Virgin Islands, sometimes referred to as the "shopping mecca of the Caribbean." With no customs duties on tourism-related products, U.S. residents are allowed a duty-free limit of $1,200 per person.

The U.S. Virgin Islands can be easily reached by airplane from all major cities in North America; the islands are connected to other islands and each other by several smaller commuter lines. Also, all the major cruise lines operate cruises here year-round, with St. Thomas holding rank as the number one cruise port in the Caribbean. Island-hopping is also easily accomplished via ferry and seaplane shuttles; a high-speed ferry connects the U.S. Virgins to Tortola and Virgin Gorda in the British Virgin Islands.

Transportation on the islands includes bus service on all but St. John, where jeep and taxi are the mode. Taxis on all three islands are fare-regulated by destination rather than mileage and, as on Puerto Rican publicos, the driver is apt to pick up passengers along the way and make stops you had not anticipated. Car rentals and mopeds are available, but remember to keep on the left side, a carry-over from Danish rule.

The weather in the Virgin Islands is always comfortable; winter averages 77 degrees and summer 82 degrees, with easterly trade winds.

Beaches on all three islands boast powdery white sand, and the right-of-access to any beach is protected by law. The turquoise, clear sea water is popular for all water sports, including windsurfing, snorkeling, catamarans, yachting, diving, and sportfishing. The U.S. Virgin Islands is one of the most popular dive areas in the world, and excellent fishing is revealed in the many world records set in these waters. Tennis, golf, horseback riding, and exploring are also tops on the recreation list.

Nightlife on St. Thomas and St. Croix is quite lively, with several hotels and some restaurants providing limbo dancers and calypso singers. The tranquil island of St. John offers no real nightlife, just quiet beauty.

For additional information on the U.S. Virgin Islands contact:

U.S. Virgin Islands Division of Tourism Office
1270 Avenue of the Americas
New York, NY 10020
(212) 582–4520; (800) USVI–INFO
or
3460 Wilshire Blvd., Suite 412
Los Angeles, CA 90010
(213) 739–0138; (800) USVI–INFO

❋

St. Thomas

The capital of the U.S. Virgin Islands, St. Thomas, is 32 miles square and is a combination of ship docks, shopping, pastel-washed, red-tiled homes clinging to green hillsides, and spectacular ocean and island vistas.

Two ocean-offerings not to be missed are in St. Thomas. Magens Bay was called by *National Geographic* "one of the ten most beautiful beaches in the world," and the small admission fee is certainly worthwhile. The calm, clear water and powdery sand of Magens Bay make it an idyllic spot for snorkeling, swimming, sunning, or renting a windsurfer or raft. Also, Coral World, a three-story underwater observation tower and marine park open to the sea, gives the visitor a chance to observe rare rainbow-colored fish and unusual coral formations. The park is one of two such offerings in the world.

St. Thomas's capital, Charlotte Amalie, is filled with interesting architecture and literally hundreds of small shops and restaurants that cater to the steady influx of cruise line passengers and other tourists. Lunch time becomes a circus in the small, crowded streets as the "food barkers" vie for attention. The narrow hillside roads of the town can prove confusing, but give dramatic views of the picturesque boat-filled bay below.

St. Thomas is not short on historic sites, many within Charlotte Amalie, including the Legislature Building, completed in 1879, the seat of the Virgin Islands legislature; the 1671 Fort Christian, the oldest standing structure on the island; 99 Steps, a reminder of the 1700s Danish builders of the city; Market Square, the slave market of the 1600s; the 1867 Government House; and Frenchtown, a Gallic colony with winding streets inhabited by descendants of the original Bretons and Normans.

The United States' influence on St. Thomas is apparent in the fast food chains and modern shopping centers around the island. Whether this is viewed as a detriment to island scenery or a nice blend of the familiar and the exotic, it is hard to dispute the natural beauty of St. Thomas.

Carnival, a colorful festival filled with festive dances, parades, and excitement, is celebrated after Easter each year. Mocko Jumbi, an elevated "spirit" on seventeen-foot-tall stilts, is the traditional symbol of the festival.

✳

Blackbeard's Castle
Box 6041, Charlotte Amalie, St. Thomas, U.S. Virgin Islands 00804

Phone: (809) 776–1234; (800) 344–5771
Key: Inn; 20 units; Expensive/Moderate CP; AE, MC, VI, DS.
Location: In town; 3 mi. to beach; 3 mi. to airport.

Not to be confused with *Blue*beard's Castle, which sits on a nearby hill, Blackbeard's itself is poised on a hill overlooking the boat-filled harbor of Charlotte Amalie. (Government Hill, to be exact, in Charlotte Amalie.) On the grounds is a watchtower which dates back to about 1679.

Though the inn is not on a beach, it more than makes up for it with charm. It also has a wonderful pool set into the hilltop, around

Blackbeard's Castle, St. Thomas

which guests can gaze out over the harbor and rooftops. All the rooms are simply yet tastefully decorated and equipped with air conditioning, telephones, and cable televisions.

Breakfast is included in the room rate, as is transportation to the beach. Blackbeard's is a very intimate inn, elegantly run by co-owners Bob Harrington and Henrique Konzen.

✳

Bluebeard's Castle
P.O. Box 7480, St. Thomas,
U.S. Virgin Islands 00801

Phone: (809) 774–1600; (800) 524–6599
Key: Historic inn; 160 units (including 95 time-share units); Deluxe/Expensive EP; Credit cards accepted.
Location: In town; 2¹/₂ mi. to beach; 3 mi. to airport.

When you first enter the town of Charlotte Amalie, your eye is immediately drawn to a complex of white buildings with bright red roofs on a prominent hilltop, holding court over the busy harbor and town. Submerged in tropical greenery is Bluebeard's Castle, a historical monument that has grown into one of the best-known resorts in the Caribbean.

A favorite of sightseers to St. Thomas, the hotel features thirty-five acres of well-manicured gardens, fresh water swimming pool, two whirlpools, tennis courts, and assorted restaurants and duty-free shops. But not to overlook its historic significance, the tourist will also find the seventeenth-century castle tower intact with its distinctive blue shutters, as well as cannons in the old fortress wall.

Although it's hardly intimate, having grown by leaps and bounds since the 1930s, Bluebeard's Castle offers attractive accommodations, a spectacular view, and an in-town location, as well as attentive, professional service, all the while keeping alive some of the flavor of its original seventeenth-century pirate days.

The guestrooms at the hotel are modern and pleasantly furnished with ceramic tile floors, coordinating tropical prints, cable televisions, rattan furnishings, and view terraces. All of the rooms are air conditioned; spacious suites feature comfortable living room areas.

✳

Bunkers' Hill View Guest House
7A Commandant Gade, St. Thomas, U.S. Virgin Islands 00801

Phone: (809) 774–8056
Key: Guest house, 15 units; Inexpensive/Inexpensive CP; MC, VI.
Location: In town; 3 mi. to beach; 3 mi. to airport.

Located at the foot of Bunker Hill in downtown Charlotte Amalie, this convenient guest house is just steps away from shops and restaurants and around the corner from a laundromat. Bunkers' Hill View also boasts some of the most reasonable lodging rates on the island, especially in off-season, and a full breakfast is included. Rates are higher in the suites and duplexes (two-bedroom suites) that provide good family accommodations.

The white with pinkish-red trim guest house, which consists of three buildings that climb the hillside, was originally built as an apart-

Bunkers' Hill View Guest House, St. Thomas

ment complex. An interesting maze of staircases unites the three buildings, all offering some hillside views.

The choice of accommodations at this bed and breakfast includes, as mentioned, guestrooms, suites, and duplexes. All of the guest accommodations have televisions, air conditioning, and inter-room phones. The only shared baths are in the two-bedroom suites, which are usually occupied by one family. These suites include a large kitchen and patio as well.

The accommodating rates at Bunkers' Hill View are matched by the very generous complimentary breakfasts served on an outside dining terrace. Bacon, eggs, toast, juice, and coffee are offered to guests as they rise between 7:30 A.M. and 10 A.M.

For other bargains offered at Bunkers' Hill guests might like to talk with manager Angela Rawlins. Ms. Rawlins is happy to arrange reductions on major car rentals and a VIP shopping and dining card with savings at certain establishments, as well as 10 percent reductions for stays of seven days at Bunkers' Hill during the summer months.

✳

Galleon House
P.O. Box 6577, St. Thomas, U.S. Virgin Islands 00801

Phone: (809) 774–6952; (800) 524–2052
Key: Inn; 14 units; Inexpensive/Inexpensive CP; AE, MC, VI, DC.
Location: In town; 3 mi. to beach; 3 mi. to airport.

This small, friendly bed and breakfast inn is just a short walk from the heart of Charlotte Amalie, at the same time affording impressive views of the harbor and the red-tiled abodes below. Several unassuming flights of stairs lead to the informal central veranda that overlooks the inn's attractive pool. Here is where guests congregate for the complimentary morning meal as well as for friendly conversation day or night.

The fourteen guestrooms are located in three buildings, an older structure and two newer buildings.

The original guestroom structure is apparent in the interesting antique molding with gold leaf designs that graces the long hallway leading to the guestrooms. In contrast, a large refrigerator is conveniently located in the same corridor to store food and cold drinks for the guests. All of the guestrooms in this building boast private baths except two. The "Prince Royal" is a favorite of honeymooners. This spacious room, with unusual "shingled" walls, king size bed, and blue and white

Galleon House, St. Thomas

accents, offers a nice, informal charm. The remainder of the guestrooms off the corridor, all named in brass plaques on the doors, are individually appointed and feature pretty printed sheets, fabric wallhangings, cheerful bedspreads, and either ceiling fans or air conditioners.

The newer buildings at the Galleon have been blended with the older structure nicely, sporting turn-of-the-century detailing and the nicest views of the harbor. These more private units have attractive ceramic tile floors, televisions, and private baths, and feature verandas with gingerbread coverings that take full advantage of the spectacular view.

The complimentary breakfast fare at the Galleon House changes each day, but includes juice or fresh fruit and French toast, pancakes, or eggs, making the already reasonable accommodations hard to beat.

❋

Hotel 1829
30 Kongens Gade, P.O. Box 1567, St. Thomas, U.S. Virgin Islands 00801

Phone: (809) 774–1829; (800) 524–2002
Key: Historic inn; 15 units; Expensive/Inexpensive EP; AE, MC, VI, DS.
Location: In town; 3 mi. to beach; 3 mi. to airport.

Located next to the historic "99 Steps" on Government Hill and a block from the main shopping streets of town, the Hotel 1829 offers superior accommodations coupled with old-world charm. The European flavor of the establishment might well be attributed to the fact that the hotel, originally a private residence, was built by a French sea captain, designed by an Italian architect in a Spanish-style motif, and constructed by Danish labor.

Careful restoration of the 1829-built inn, in operation since 1939, shows in every detail. The salmon-pink structure with green awnings is located on a steep grade and is part of the city's historic walking tour. The brick-step entry leads to wrought-iron gates that open to massive wooden doors at the top. The front entry is actually the terrace dining area, with comfortable rattan tables and chairs, thick wooden shutters, planters over-brimming with red poinsettias, and a tranquil fountain.

The fifteen guest accommodations on different levels are positioned around an interior courtyard that is every bit as charming as the exterior. Victorian benches, occasional antique cupboards and sideboards, and "tulip-shaped," turn-of-the-century lighting fixtures grace the exposed corridors as bougainvillea drapes colorfully over the brick walls.

The guestrooms themselves are all different, ranging from moderate poolside rooms to deluxe rooms and suites overlooking St. Thomas' boat-filled harbor. The suites and deluxe accommodations feature queen size beds, HBO color television, completely outfitted wet bars, and private balconies. The more moderately priced rooms are nestled around the pool and terrace, but all the guestrooms feature such special touches as rich terra-cotta tile (that blends nicely with the 200-year-old Moroccan tile in the dining area), air conditioning, warm brick-exposed walls, wooden-shuttered windows, coordinated fabrics and designer sheets, and stained-glass accents. All accommodations have private baths with ultra-modern fixtures and ceramic tile.

The 1829 Restaurant is highly regarded on the island for its seafood dishes and tasty desserts.

The bar of Hotel 1829 was the original Dutch kitchen with the old Dutch oven intact, the 200-year-old floors, and special touches such as stained glass and games for guests. The hotel registration is handled here by an efficient and pleasant staff.

✳

Island View Guest House
P.O. Box 1903, St. Thomas, U.S. Virgin Islands 00801

Phone: (809) 774–4270; (800) 524–2023
Key: Guest house; 15 units; Inexpensive/Inexpensive CP; AE, MC, VI.
Location: Near town; 2 mi. to beach; 2 mi. to airport.

Situated midway between the airport and Charlotte Amalie on a secluded and lush tropical hillside, 545 feet above St. Thomas's harbor, is the Island View Guest House. The casual and private spot on Crown Mountain offers a reasonable vacation and friendly environs.

The neat, blue and white, thirty-two-year-old concrete building was originally a private home; it was nicely converted to a guest house in 1969. Hospitable managers Barbara Cooper and Norman Leader have kept guests at Island View contented and the establishment well maintained for twelve years now.

The main floor of the bed and breakfast features the "Gallery," the hub of guest activity that overlooks the attractive pool and the town

Island View Guest House, St. Thomas

and harbor in a breathtaking way. Guests enjoy comfortable lounging in the spacious room with several small conversation areas as well as an extensive honor bar. The complimentary morning fare consisting of toast, juice and coffee is served in the "Gallery" between 8 and 9:30 A.M. For bigger appetites a full breakfast is available at a modest charge. Sandwiches are prepared for lunch, and for dinner, there is a brand new dining room where guests can feast on West Indian, Continental, and German dishes prepared by the German chef.

The pleasant and cheerful guestrooms at Island View include eight rooms plus a suite in the original part of the building and six rooms in a new addition. The latter can be rented with or without a kitchen. All accommodations boast views of the harbor and are furnished modestly but pleasantly, with pretty bedspreads and shower curtains and absolute cleanliness. The recently remodeled suite features a large terrace and sleeps four.

The large pool with pretty tile and a spacious sundeck surrounding it clings to the steep hillside and affords the same spectacular views. Please note that although an unobtrusive railing on the cliff side of the guest house provides adequate safety for the inn's adult guests, it is not an ideal situation for small children. For this reason Island View does not accept children under fourteen years of age. The guest house provides complimentary beach towels and rents snorkel gear for a small fee.

❋

Maison Greaux Guest House
23 Solberg, P.O. Box 1856, St. Thomas,
U.S. Virgin Islands 00801

Phone: (809) 774–0063
Key: Guest house; 10 units; Inexpensive/Inexpensive CP; MC, VI.
Location: Near town; 3 mi. to beach; 3 mi. to airport.

Tucked away on a quiet, residential cul-de-sac 600 feet above town is this three-story, thirty-four-year-old white guest house with yellow trim. A small sidewalk lined with coconut palms and tropical plants and flowers surrounds the building; a staircase climb leads to the outdoor terrace/lounge—a friendly gathering place for the bed and breakfast guests.

The outside terrace, cooled by pleasant breezes and furnished with simple tables and chairs, offers a television, a popular honor bar, and spectacular 180-degree views of Charlotte Amalie and the harbor. The complimentary continental breakfast consisting of orange juice, coffee, and Danish pastry or French croissants is served here between 7:30 A.M. and 9:00 A.M. by the congenial owners, Irene and Richard Cline. On-season breakfasts may occasionally be more elaborate.

The ten guestrooms are all different, and five have private baths. Six of the ten guest accommodations offer air conditioning; the others

Maison Greaux Guest House, St. Thomas

are cooled by trade winds and ceiling fans.

Maison Greaux is only minutes from downtown shopping and restaurants in its secluded residential area, and it is convenient to ferry and seaplane shuttles.

✳

Miller Manor Guest House
27 & 28 Princesse Gade, P.O. Box 1570, St. Thomas, U.S. Virgin Islands 00801

Phone: (809) 774–1535
Key: Guest house; 22 units; Inexpensive/Inexpensive EP; No credit cards; No children under 4–5.
Location: In town; 3 mi. to beach; 3 mi. to airport.

Once a private home, the immaculate and homey 120-year-old Danish townhouse has expanded to a second building to house guests in both comfortable guesthouses and full apartments. The pale yellow hillside home is accented with attractive white Grecian columns. A white iron gate and a patio entry with a profusion of tropical plants keep the guest house private even though it is just a short walk from town.

The parlor of the old house reflects the warmth of its owners for over thirty-five years, the Millers. Decorated in comfortable antiques and memorabilia, the room is separated from the adjacent dining room by a wide, open arch. The formal dining room, not used by guests for actual dining, adds to the atmosphere of the establishment with its interesting lincrusta ceiling, ornate crystal chandelier, and pretty antique furnishings. The polished ceramic floors of the two common rooms, along with paintings, fresh flowers, and lots of reading material, make the area as inviting as "grandmother's" home. Directly off the formal dining room of the house is a large veranda offering beautiful views of the harbor. Although no meals are offered at Miller Manor, guests are enrolled in the "Bottle Club" and may stock their own liquor to go with the plentiful mixes provided there.

Proceeding down a short, steep staircase from the main floor, you will discover 120-year-old brick pillars and arches of the house and a rooftop terrace lounging area with guestrooms and apartments nearby.

The guestrooms and apartments at Miller Manor include a few antique-decorated rooms in the old house and more contemporary furnishings in the five-story newer structure. Overall, the furnishings are cheerful and comfortable with pretty curtains and bedspreads, and the rooms are extremely clean. All of the homey accommodations boast private baths and many of the rooms are quite spacious. Some of the apartments, which are ideal for families, have full kitchens, two complete bedrooms, and living room. Rates on apartments are also very reasonable.

This well-manicured bargain with homestyle atmosphere fills up sometimes a year in advance, so try to reserve early. Aida Miller, the manager/owner, takes delight in seeing her many friends who return each year, some for more than thirty-five years now.

✳

Also on the Island

Point Pleasant
Estate Smith Bay #4, St. Thomas,
U.S. Virgin Islands 00802

Phone: (809) 775–7200
Representative: Robert Reid Associates

Point Pleasant is indeed pleasant. Perched on top of a bluff on the northeast side of the island, it surveys the sea, dotted with islands and sparkling white sailboats. Its accommodations (a total of 134 suites of varying sizes, all with kitchens) are decorated with rattan furniture, floral fabrics, and straw tile rugs. Each has a terrace with a gorgeous view of the sea. There are three pools, a tennis court, wooded trails for strolling, and a private beach. Its Agave Terrace Restaurant is highly respected on the island.

✳

St. Croix

The largest island in the U.S. Virgins, St. Croix totals eighty-four square miles of mostly hilly terrain with pastures and tropical foliage and has two main towns, Christiansted and Frederiksted. Christiansted, the one-time Danish West Indies capital, founded in 1734, is a National Historic Site and charms the visitor with its old-world architecture and reminders of the history. The town lies in a reef-sheltered bay surrounded by hills and boasts an abundant amount of restored Danish structures. Well-preserved Fort Christiansvaern was built in 1749 of Danish ballast. Other preserved examples to view include the Old Danish Customs House, the Scale House, and the Governor's House. The small streets of town are lined with quaint boutiques and cafes, and alley-tucked arcades provide more of the same. World famous Buck Island Reef, a glass-bottomed boat ride from town, is the only U.S. National Monument that is underwater. The park includes 850 acres with sandy beaches and a reef with two major underwater trails.

Frederiksted is a picturesque harbor town that is characterized by largely Victorian architecture due to a fire in the late 1800s that destroyed most of the original Danish Colonial buildings in town. The town, which greets cruise ship passengers who visit the island, is renovating many of its quaint, gingerbreaded buildings. There are a handful of sights to see, including Fort Frederik (which dates back to 1760), the Market Place (in operation since 1751), an aquarium, and four historic churches.

The visitor to St. Croix will not only enjoy boundless recreation, but also the green countryside filled with historic sugar mill ruins. Visitors may view the Whim Greathouse, a restored 1700s plantation, and the St. George Botanical Garden, consisting of 160 acres of lush woods and rich land, along with the ruins of an eighteenth-century sugar cane village and rum factory.

✳

Pink Fancy
27 Prince Street, Christiansted, St. Croix,
U.S. Virgin Islands 00820

Phone: (809) 773–8460; (800) 524–2045
Key: Historic inn; 13 units; Moderate/Inexpensive CP; MC, VI.
Location: In town; 2 blocks to harbor/beach; 8 mi. to airport.

Undoubtedly one of the most charming inns in the Caribbean, the Pink Fancy offers historic charm, modern amenities, and in-town convenience along with guest house friendliness and security. The small hotel, owned and meticulously renovated by Sam Dillon, incorporates four small buildings that take up most of a corner block a few streets away from the downtown boutiques and seaplane launch. The picturesque, weathered brick walls and arches are topped by a white-shin-

Pink Fancy, St. Croix

gled second story that features pastel-pink wooden shutters and small-paned windows. As you enter through the ornamental and privacy-conscious black iron gates to the brick arcade entrance, you first note the well-earned plaque on the wall reading "Pink Fancy, 1780—Registered in the National Register of Historic Places . . . 1966." This building, offering several of the thirteen guest accommodations, was once a 1780 Danish townhouse, and the remaining three buildings, focused on an attractive central courtyard, were constructed in 1880.

When Mr. Dillon acquired the property several years ago he chose to restore its 1950s use as a lodging establishment (then a haven for many famous artists and writers), but not before investing over $1 million into the careful renovation program. Saving the original walls and structures themselves, Dillon created guestroom accommodations of varying proportions within the four historic buildings. Although individually decorated, each of the guestrooms has the same airy, fresh feel created by the use of white on the walls, on the quaintly shuttered windows, and on the chenille bedspreads. The effect is dramatized by the use of tropical prints, pretty brick or walnut flooring, and luscious pink towels in the baths. Each guestroom features a comfortable sitting area, a compact efficiency kitchen (often cleverly hidden by French doors) with all the necessities, and air conditioning and fans. In addition, each room has a clock radio, color television, telephone, and modern, spacious baths with tub/shower combinations. Because of its odd shape, one unit features a corner tub that has a spa look.

The names of guestrooms were derived from old estates on the island and, at the same time, seem to apply nicely to a stay at this intimate inn. You might like to try the "Morning Star," the "Bonne Esperance," the "Work and Rest," "Recovery Hill," or "Hard Labor." If you can't identify which room you want by name alone, then note that "Work and Rest" might be combined with "Recovery Hill" for a spacious suite with antique corner nook and reading tables and batik prints. "Hard Labor" is the largest guestroom, with attractive slanted ceilings that follow the roofline, and the "Parasol" is a more intimate unit near the gazebo with views of the pool.

The small grounds of the inn are well utilized with pretty gardens and a protected courtyard with inviting pool and large palm. In this area the guest will enjoy the "Limetree Bar," the self-service complimentary bar that is well stocked and used freely by guests. The bar is also the site of the complimentary morning fare, consisting of Danish, orange juice, coffee, milk, or tea. Guests are free to enjoy the breakfast outside on the patio or in the privacy of their rooms. Next door to the bar is the office that contains a small library for guests' use. Just above the courtyard are smaller sitting areas terraced on various levels. A gazebo area offers attractive outside relaxing, and a side patio is a favorite site for impromptu barbecues organized by the guests.

Assistant manager Eustace Simon knows the inn from the inside out, having worked on the hotel from the beginning of its renovation. He, like the rest of the staff at the hotel, reflects a well-deserved pride in the establishment and is eager to share his enthusiasm with guests. Eustace is quick to point out the personal nature of the inn, where "guests all know each other within twenty-four hours—unless they want their privacy." Both attitudes are readily respected at the Pink Fancy.

※

Sprat Hall Plantation
P.O. Box 695, Frederiksted, St. Croix,
U.S. Virgin Islands 00840

Phone: (809) 772–0305; (800) 843–3584
Key: Plantation; 25 units; Expensive/Moderate CP or EP; No credit cards; Smoking ok (except great house).
Location: 200 yds. to beach; 1 mi. to town; 7 mi. to airport.

Not only is the Sprat Hall Plantation the oldest great house in the Virgin Islands and the only French plantation house left intact, it also holds the impressive title of the oldest building in private hands in the Caribbean. The majestic white great house, surrounded by pastoral scenery, was built in 1670 by French colonists who constructed it exactly like a house in Brittany. In fact, a guest of the historic inn experienced a real case of déjà vu when he arrived at the plantation on vacation, sight unseen, to discover it the duplicate of his own home in Brittany—the original great house upon which Sprat Hall was modeled. Owners Judy and Mark Young, whose families have been in St. Croix since the 1700s, will happily tell you this and more about the history of Sprat Hall and the island they call their home.

The plantation, consisting of over twenty acres of pasture, five acres of lawn, ancient trees, and flowering shrubs, is a serene country inn that offers the only riding stables in the Virgin Islands. Part of the acreage at Sprat Hall Plantation is devoted to raising the fresh fruit and vegetables used to make the wonderful homemade food served at the inn.

Guests arrive at the plantation by way of a lazy country road flanked by bright flamboyant trees. The only sounds are of the long-tailed green parrots or cockatoos that populate the country terrain or the knoll-top breeze that carries the soothing rhythm of the waves 200 yards away. The gracious great house greets you on its hilltop with views of the sea and hills for miles. Lazy trees, potted plants, and palms surround the structure with curved-arch gallery, green wooden shutters, and old stone steps. An Oriental carpet in greens and blues ushers the guest into the parlor, the original dining room of the house. The parlor, enjoyed by guests, has light blue walls with white trim and is furnished in an interesting combination of antiques. A built-in hutch holds books, a television is cleverly blended with the old, and the result is both comfort and a fascinating touch of the past.

The dining room, adjacent to the parlor, is one of the two restaurants of the inn. The other is the more informal beachfront eatery a few hundred yards away. This formal dining room, the original ballroom of the great house, features a blue and white Royal Copenhagen decor from the elegant table china to the draperies tied back at the windows. The room is all antique with old wooden floors, another built-in china hutch with antique glass pieces, and antique mahogany tables and chairs. Nighttime diners are treated to candlelight supplied by individual hurricane holders and candelabra that surround the room. All three meals are served at the plantation, with an emphasis on homemade and homegrown.

A bar is located at the rear, bottom level of the house and is a

Sprat Hall Plantation, St. Croix

casual gathering spot. Upstairs are the four guestrooms of the great house, each a study in antique history and very individual. These prized rooms are not offered to smokers or children, with good reason. Behind each door is a bevy of one-of-a-kind antique beds and family mementos that have been lovingly restored by the family. One room features French antiques and has the only original great house antique, an ornately carved pineapple canopy bed. A cane settee and twin rockers, a marble writing table, and an armoire are set off by the pink walls, green shutters, and large pink and green woven rug. The other three guestrooms, all with private bath, include a "Danish" room, an "English" room, and a small single room decorated in a family member's antique furnishings, keepsakes, and photographs.

The remainder of the guest accommodations at the plantation are located in a 1948-built, two-story structure, in 1969-constructed bungalows, and also in two-, three- and four-bedroom houses. These other guest lodgings are decorated in more modern furnishings of rattan or teak and color-coordinated fabrics.

Over forty years of owner-management of the Sprat Hall Plantation have perfected the informal and congenial atmosphere of the inn. Whether lounging on the beach a short stroll away, horseback riding through the plantation's rain forest, or soaking up local history, the guest will find this historic inn a relaxing country retreat.

※

Villa Madeleine
P.O. Box 24190, Teague Bay, St. Croix,
U.S. Virgin Islands 00824

Phone: (809) 773–8141; (800) 548–4461
Key: Inn; 20 units; Deluxe/Deluxe EP; AE, MC, VI, DS.
Location: 10 minutes east of Christiansted.

One of the island's newest accommodations (opened in 1990), Villa Madeleine offers a beautiful collection of one- and two-bedroom villas. Each one has a complete kitchen, a large marble bathroom, and a private walled patio with a plunge pool. Inside, there are all sorts of fine details, such as intricate woodwork and mahogany French doors. Decor is airy and tropical with pastel colors and wicker and rattan furniture, including four-poster rattan beds. All have stunning sea views.

The main building, which is propped up on a hill, was modeled after a plantation great house. It's elegantly furnished with Oriental rugs and antique pieces. A sitting room, a library, and a billiard room, along with Cafe Madeleine, the hotel's Italian restaurant, are all available at the hotel. The restaurant has rapidly become known as one of the best—if not *the* best—restaurant on the island. Diners can choose between the canopied veranda overlooking the sea or the air-conditioned dining room, which is elegantly appointed with antiques and plants.

There are complete water and land sports available nearby, including tennis courts and a golf course.

✳

Also on the Island

Anchor Inn
58-A King Street, Christiansted, St. Croix,
U.S. Virgin Islands 00820

Phone: (809) 773–4000; (800) 524–2030

Directly on the waterfront in the heart of downtown Christiansted is this thirty-guestroom inn with small swimming pool and popular terraced restaurant. The inn is also accessible off the main shopping street, down one of the town's hidden alleyways. The U-shaped, two-story complex is in intimate quarters, giving it a rather European feel. Guest accommodations include twin beds, color television, refrigerator, bath, air conditioning, telephone, and small balconies. Suites offer double beds, but no balconies. The decor is fairly similar in all the rooms, offering contemporary, pleasant furnishings in an orange motif. The restaurant serves all meals and features continental and West Indian cuisine.

Club Comanche
1 Strand Street, Christiansted, St. Croix,
U.S. Virgin Islands 00820

Phone: (809) 773–0210

Located in the very heart of downtown, surrounded by the quaint boutiques of a popular alley shopping arcade, is the Club Comanche with its notable hydraulic caged elevator, awning-covered bridge that spans tiny Strand Street, and unique guestroom offerings. Guest accommodations at the forty-six-unit inn include impressive split-level suites, four-posters, and antiques and more contemporary units. The "landmark" accommodation of the Club is the Mill Room, which is actually a restored sugar mill that has been converted to a tri-plex guest suite right on the water's edge. Two restaurants, one inside the hotel and the other on the terrace, offer excellent dining and a lengthy wine list.

✺

St. John

The smallest of the inhabited U.S. Virgins with only twenty-eight square miles of territory, St. John is perhaps the loveliest with its verdant, mountainous landscape surrounded by sugar-white beaches and tourmaline sea. Due to Laurance Rockefeller's foresight and generosity, more than two-thirds of the island is overseen by the National Park Service for perpetual safekeeping and preservation. This 7,028-acre preserve offers beaches with panoramic views, woodland trails, and wildlife sanctuaries, as well as spectacular underwater trails at Trunk Bay that delight snorkelers.

Although St. John may certainly be a travel destination by itself, many visitors from St. Thomas arrive for the day. A pleasant, double-decker ferry from St. Thomas's Red Hook dock arrives in St. John's Cruz Bay on a frequent daily schedule. The ride, with gorgeous island and ocean views included, takes only twenty minutes and is one of the best bargains in the U.S. Virgin Islands! Cruz Bay is a cute little town with a small square and two shopping complexes—Mongoose Junction and Wharfside Village—crammed with shops and restaurants. The shops offer some good Caribbean artwork, pottery, handcrafted gold and silver jewelry, blown glass, and hand-painted T-shirts and dresses. In town, taxis, which are really open-air trucks equipped with benches and red- and white-striped awnings, take visitors on island tours and to various beaches. The cost is reasonable, but jeeps and mopeds may also be rented here.

Trunk Bay is probably the most popular tourist destination on the island with its crystal-clear water and underwater trails. A good hamburger stand is there, as are changing rooms, bathrooms, and outdoor showers.

✳

Caneel Bay
St. John, U.S. Virgin Islands 00830

Phone: (809) 776–6111; (800) 223–7637
Reservations: Rockresorts Reservations
Key: Inn; 171 units; Deluxe/Deluxe EP; AE, VI, DC, MC.
Location: On beach; 2 mi. to town.

This full resort facility that caters to the wealthy, honeymooners, or those seeking a relaxing off-season bargain in luxury has developed on 170 acres of scenic land filled with beautifully maintained tropical gardens, seven white-sand beaches, and the remains of the eighteenth-century sugar mill (now a restaurant).

Guests at Caneel Bay have the lovely option of being active every moment or not doing anything at all in this serene former plantation environment. Activities, all included in your stay, can include tennis at one of the seven courts, sailing, swimming, snorkeling or scuba in the clear waters, sightseeing excursions, and more. Or for pure relaxation, the guest at Caneel Bay may choose to stroll around the beautiful grounds and take in the surrounding hills of the Virgin Islands National Park or just laze on one of the comfortable lounges on the beach of his or her choice.

At Caneel Bay guests may dine atop an eighteenth-century sugar mill, on a terrace overlooking the ocean, or on the patio of a restored manor house. The inn's Sugar Mill restaurant is one of the three dining spots and is popular with the day visitors who stop for lunch. A delightful patio bar offers nighttime entertainment. Full American meal plans (including all three meals) and Modified American meal plans (including breakfast and dinner) are available.

The guestrooms at the plantation range from tennis garden rooms that are situated away from the bay to the most expensive premium rooms that are situated along the beach. The rooms are all fairly spacious and attractively decorated in contemporary furnishings with natural color tones. The serenity of the getaway resort is insured with a lack of television or telephone (sound-proofed public phones are located near the reception area). Ceiling fans provide adequate ventilation as do the louvers and patio doors. As a nice touch, a welcoming bottle of Virgin Island rum awaits the guest upon checking in.

While Caneel Bay is far from an intimate resort in terms of size, it has the space and peacefulness that allow for an intimate stay. Personal service is not easy to achieve with the brisk business that goes on here even if off-season, but professional service is a requirement at this popular resort on one of the loveliest islands in the Caribbean.

*

Villa Bougainvillea
P.O. Box 349, Cruz Bay, St. John,
U.S. Virgin Islands 00830

Phone: (809) 776–6420 (days); (809) 776–6856; or (800) 253–7107
Key: House; 2 units; Expensive/Moderate EP; AE, MC, VI, DS.
Location: In town; ¹/₂ block to beach; 4 blocks to seaplane.

Brilliant red and purple bougainvillea frame the porch views at this private villa on a hillside in Cruz Bay. The two-story house offers a separate apartment on each of its two levels and is set within a landscaped, stone-walled garden.

The first-floor apartment offers two bedrooms—a master room with queen bed and a second with a double bed. A modern kitchen is fully supplied for cooking. Distinctive fieldstone walls are found in the apartment's living room/dining room area and in the adjacent outdoor

Villa Bougainvillea, St. John

porch with sofa, chairs, and hanging flowers and vines.

The second-floor apartment boasts panoramic views of the sea and neighboring islands and two bedrooms as well. One bedroom offers a twin bed, and the large master bedroom has a king size bed. The living room, with stereo, teakwood furnishings, and original art, opens onto a deck through sliding glass doors. The fully-equipped kitchen features attractive stained-glass windows.

Both apartments come equipped with ceiling fans, all linens and towels, quality furnishings, and special touches such as garden bouquets throughout the house. Each apartment at Villa Bougainvillea sleeps up to five people, with children welcome, and special monthly rates are available. Villa Bougainvillea's owners, Donald and Deborah Schnell, are island residents on hand to see to your needs personally, and, as a special hospitable gesture, offer complimentary tropical cocktails at the Mongoose Restaurant or at the Fern House Restaurant to all guests of the Villa.

This convenient location requires no vehicle for most activities since it is within walking distance to town shops, restaurants, taxi "trucks," and the seaplane launch.

British Virgin Islands

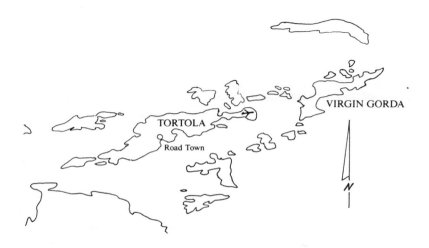

TORTOLA

Road Town

VIRGIN GORDA

N

*L*ong known as a sailors' paradise, this small archipelago is slowly being discovered by *terra firma* visitors. More than fifty islands, rocks, and cays situated in these incredibly clear, turquoise waters form the British Virgin Islands, although many of these volcano-produced formations are uninhabited. Best known in the British Virgin Islands are Tortola and Virgin Gorda; less talked about islands include Jost Van Dyke, Norman Island, Peter Island, Salt Island, and Beef Island, which connects to Tortola by bridge and is the site of the British Virgin Island's airport. Anegada is the only coral (non-volcanic) and flat island in the chain. The rest are made up of hills.

Getting to these islands, located just sixty miles east of Puerto Rico, is easy by air, although non-stop flights are not available. Daily connections from St. Thomas, St. Croix, and Puerto Rico, as well as connections from other Caribbean islands, are plentiful. High-speed ferry services connecting Tortola, Virgin Gorda, St. Thomas, and St. John are numerous. A small departure tax is collected when leaving these islands. The U.S. dollar is the official currency, and the language is English. A passport, birth certificate, or voter's registration card is sufficient for entry here. The British Virgin Islands are on Atlantic Standard Time (one hour earlier than Eastern Standard Time), except during Daylight Saving season when clocks in these islands are the same as those in the Eastern U.S.

Recreation equals water-related sports and leisure in the British Virgin Islands. The clear, calm waters and protected cays and coves make sailing, windsurfing, scuba, and snorkeling extraordinary. Fishing is considered excellent, but the colorful tropical fish are not to be caught and, like the coral, are for "looking" only. Hundreds of uncrowded, white sandy beaches make relaxing and shell collecting favorite activities in these islands. Divers enjoy their sport here year-round with visibility of 50 to 100 feet or more.

The hilly terrain, ancient ruins of sugar mills, pirate caves, and rain forests make hiking, bird-watching, and exploring popular pastimes, as are golf, tennis and horseback riding. The nightlife on the islands is restricted mainly to informal gatherings in open-air bars and restaurants.

For more information on the British Virgin Islands contact:

British Virgin Island Tourist Board
370 Lexington Avenue
New York, NY 10017
(800) 232–7770; (212) 696–0400

or

British Virgin Islands Tourist Board
1686 Union Street
San Francisco, CA 94123
(800) 232–7770; (415) 775–0344

✳

Tortola

This twelve-mile-long by three-mile-wide island has a population of about 10,000 and contains the capital of the islands, Road Town, where the main shops, banks, hospital, and government buildings are located. The southern shore of the island has jagged mountain peaks rising over 1,700 feet, and the northern shore boasts white, powdery beaches and tropical groves. The Mount Sage National Park offers glimpses of a primeval rain forest on its slopes.

Although tourism has increased in the last twenty years with the advent of additional hostelries, Tortola is still a rural, slow-paced island with marauding goats, lambs, and chickens and friendly people. Shopping is still minimal; local shops are located in or near Road Town. Car rental agencies are plentiful, especially in town, but note that neither car rental companies nor shops are open on Sunday.

Connected by the 300-foot Queen Elizabeth Bridge is the small Beef Island, a hunting ground during the pirate days, now providing airport service to the islands. Near Beef Island is Marina Cay, a six-acre island brought to fame by the book and movie entitled *Our Virgin Island*.

✳

Fort Recovery
P.O. Box 239, Road Town, Tortola,
British Virgin Islands

Phone: (809) 495–4467; (800) 367–8455
Key: Inn; 10 units; Moderate/Moderate EP; AE.
Location: On beach; 7 mi. to town; 16 mi. to airport.

This is not really an inn, but a small assemblage of villas that surround an original seventeenth-century Dutch fort of the same name.

Fort Recovery, Tortola

Fort Recovery offers ten completely equipped villas that are rented mainly by the week, but are sometimes available for shorter periods. Their location is idyllically private and quiet, off the main road from town and fronting an intimate, private beach and small boat dock. The grounds themselves add to the overall tranquility with ample bougainvillea, oleander, and hibiscus around the grassy areas dotted with palms.

Each unit is very private, with its own semi-enclosed patio draped in purple bougainvillea, fully equipped kitchen, spacious living room, and separate bedroom; each bedroom boasts a separate entrance as well. All the villas are air conditioned and decorated tastefully, and maid service is provided daily. There are eight one-bedroom villas, one two-bedroom villa, and one four-bedroom house. The property is very well run by the original owner—Anita MacShane—and her island staff.

For the traveler in need of a little rest and relaxation, coupled with modern comforts and quiet, Fort Recovery certainly lives up to its name. What could be more restful than listening to the waves lap gently a few feet away and watching the sailboats, silhouetted against the nearby islands, glide by all day long?

Long Bay Beach Resort
P.O. Box 433, Road Town, Tortola,
British Virgin Islands

Phone: (809) 495–4252; (800) 729–9599
Key: Inn; 70 units; Deluxe/Expensive MAP; AE, MC, VI.
Location: On beach; 10 mi. to town; 19 mi. to airport.

Since recently expanding, the Long Bay Beach Resort is not an inn per se. However, it does have an inn-like intimacy. Its seventy units are spread around the complex and are either built into the hillside or strung along the chlorine-white beach.

The landscaped estate has a private club feel from the moment you enter the grounds. The ruins of an old sugar mill containing an informal restaurant greet you. Guests may have breakfast, luncheon, or dinner here within the sugar mill walls or on the patios that extend to the white sand beyond. The menus are more causal here than in the main dining room, but very tasty, with banana pancake breakfasts or curry dinners. The inviting swimming pool is a step away from the restaurant, and the beach, complete with comfortable lounges, is only a few yards away.

A lazy country road leads the guest to the tennis courts of the

Long Bay Beach Resort, Tortola

95

resort as well as the nine-hole pitch and putt gold course. Just a short stroll across the road is the other dining room of the hotel and bar just below. Guests are treated to a daily selected menu here in a more formal atmosphere. The bar is a gathering and socializing spot for guests in the evening. Children are discouraged in the main dining room, but the hosts are happy to arrange babysitting.

The guest accommodations at Long Bay can suit about any taste, ranging from complete two-bedroom villas with kitchens and living rooms to standard twin-bedded rooms with balcony overlooking the ocean. The beachfront cabanas feature an elevated bedroom with twin beds, kitchenette, and sundeck as well as covered patio on the sand. Furnishings include nicely tiled, modern bathrooms and attractive decor featuring rattan, wicker, tropical prints, and windows that take advantage of the inspiring views.

This quiet escape has a friendly, safe feel that enables the guest to wander the countrified grounds day and night without hesitation.

✳

Sebastian's on the Beach
Little Apple Bay, P.O. Box 441, Road Town, Tortola, British Virgin Islands

Phone: (809) 495–4212; (800) 336–4870
Key: Inn; 26 units; Moderate/Inexpensive EP; AE.
Location: On beach; 10 mi. to town; 19 mi. to airport.

Located on a scenic stretch of beach at Little Apple Bay is this popular, informal inn consisting of beachfront, modern rooms, and an older complex across the road that houses guestrooms as well as a store with an interesting medley of groceries, souvenirs, and supplies. The active spot attracts its share of surfers in the winter when surf at the hotel draws aficionados from Hawaii and New Zealand to Sebastian's.

The guestrooms in the newer complex that nearly touches the surf are nicely decorated in coordinated rattan furnishings with flowered bedspreads and attractive wood-beamed ceilings. The rooms boast modern, private baths with showers, mini-refrigerators, and airy, spacious square footage. Some of these accommodations in the contemporary two-story buildings have views of the ocean, while others face the central courtyard where the activity seems to gravitate. More moderately priced accommo-

Sebastian's on the Beach, Tortola

dations are offered in the maroon-colored structure just across the road.

The restaurant at Sebastian's offers simple fare—mainly grilled fish dishes—and is so popular, reservations are a must (the day's selection is posted on a chalkboard at the store desk). The combined restaurant and guest lounge has comfortable seating, nautical decor, and an adjoining beachside patio. Breakfast and lunch are also offered in the open-air bistro at moderate prices.

Sebastian's on the Beach offers an informal, beach-oriented stay for those who seek the company of fellow guests and the sounds of the waves a few feet away. It is the kind of cozy spot you can visit with just a bathing suit for daytime and, not much fancier, for night and be right in style.

✻

Sugar Mill Hotel
Apple Bay, P.O. Box 425, Road Town, Tortola,
British Virgin Islands

Phone: (809) 495–4355; (800) 462–8834
Representative: Caribbean Inns, Ltd.
Key: Historic inn; 20 units; Expensive/Moderate EP; AE, VI, MC.
Location: 75 yd. to beach; 9 mi. to town; 18 mi. to airport.

Take two travel and food writers from California who long to experience the romanticism of innkeeping from the other side of the typewriter and add one quaint, historic inn and restaurant on a beautiful Caribbean island; the result is the Sugar Mill Hotel—a pleasant blend of island informality and romantic charm. That is how owners Jinx and Jeff Morgan recall their advent into innkeeping, and the resultant inn and gourmet restaurant reflect their sophisticated touches and good humor in many delightful ways.

The Sugar Mill Hotel was originally a 1600s sugar mill plantation built from the stone and brick ballast from British ships. At the entrance to the hillside grounds are the walls of the sugar mill and rum distillery; the ancient walls have been used to house the main dining area of the hotel. The restaurant, which has won wide acclaim, features a spacious open-air pavilion with tropical planter. There is also a more intimate dining terrace with undisturbed views of the ocean just across the road. Both have views enhanced by the tropical flora that covers the estate. The terrace with comfortable straw seating, tropical birds that patrol for crumbs from the rafters, and the old stone walls is a delightful breakfast spot. A large silver urn holds help-yourself coffee, a doily-lined basket serves up homebaked muffins and coconut bread, and individually formed butter patties are placed lovingly next to the homemade jelly. It is a congenial spot where guests compare travel notes, and the resident dog and cat wander by to say good morning. Reservations are taken for the four-course dinners with varying menus that are served each night.

Drinks are enjoyed in the adjacent bar stocked with reading material as well as at the pool honor bar behind the restaurant. Luncheon is served at the dining patio on the Sugar Mill beach a few steps away. The sign here sets the mood: it requests visitors to "kick off your shoes" and relax. Lounge chairs and tables set with crisp blue tablecloths are provided for hamburger, sandwich, or lobster salad mid-day dining. A small sandy beach is inviting for a swim or lounging or as a backdrop to dining.

The guest accommodations at the inn, consisting of a mixture of wood-sided bungalow buildings and contemporary stucco structures with arches and patios, are nestled around the grounds between the hibiscus and various tropical trees. The modern suites, cottages, and studio apartments, set against the lush hills, all offer panoramic views of the ocean. The interior decor is neat, clean, and attractive. The Morgans have been gradually upgrading the guestrooms, adding cozy plants, small libraries, fresh bedspreads, and island watercolor paintings.

A circular swimming pool lined in pretty blue tile is inviting and boasts an "over the rooftops" view of the ocean. A plentiful supply of lounges and Ping-Pong are provided here for guests' enjoyment.

Also on the Island

Frenchman's Cay Resort Hotel
P.O. Box 1054, West End, Tortola,
British Virgin Islands

Phone: (809) 495–4844; (800) 235–4077

Tucked away on the west end of Tortola, Frenchman's Cay Resort Hotel is a collection of nine one- and two-bedroom villas. Each one has a kitchen, a dining room, a sitting room, and a terrace. There are also a restaurant and bar, a pool, a beach, and a tennis court.

Moorings-Mariner Inn
P.O. Box 139, Road Town, Tortola,
British Virgin Islands

Phone: (809) 494–2332

Anyone who has ever been to the British Virgin Islands knows the Moorings. It's the hub of sailing activity on Tortola and attracts sloops with flags from around the world. All forty guestrooms are simple yet pleasant, with ceiling fans and private terraces (many overlooking the marina). Here, life revolves largely around the boats, the bar, and the pool. There is also a tennis court.

Treasure Isle Hotel
P.O. Box 68, Road Town, Tortola,
British Virgin Islands

Phone: (809) 494–2501

This hotel near Road Town has an inviting swimming pool with porthole views of the ocean and a pleasant outdoor dining terrace, as well as tennis and marina facilities. All forty guestrooms are air conditioned and have telephones. The hotel offers complimentary beach trips to different island beaches and to the hotel's beach club on Cooper Island.

✳

Virgin Gorda

This rural, quiet island is characterized by mountains in the north and flat, dry land with giant boulders, scrub, and cactus in the south. Exploration highlights include an abandoned copper mine, about twenty beautiful turquoise and white sands beaches, and a unique rock formation called The Baths, which consists of huge boulders with sea caves that are dimly lit by sunlight filtering through.

Virgin Gorda, with a modest population of about 1,400, is a popular stop-over for sightseers and the yachting set. Daytrippers can take a twenty-minute ferry from Tortola and dock right at Yacht Harbour. A few small boutiques and pubs are located right at the harbor, and Little Dix Bay is a pleasant walk away.

Everything is still very low-key on the island, and although Little Dix Bay was established as an exclusive resort in 1964, tourism did not really hit the island until about fifteen years ago. Other than by foot, getting around the island can be accomplished by car rental or by taxi, but beware of the expense of hiring a taxi and discuss the rate first.

✳

Olde Yard Inn
P.O. Box 26, Virgin Gorda, British Virgin Islands

Phone: (809) 495–5544; (800) 633–7411
Key: Inn; 14 units; Expensive/Moderate EP; VI, MC.
Location: ¹/₄ mi. to beach, ¹/₂ mi. to town; ¹/₂ mi. to airport.

The Olde Yard Inn is the kind of hotel you discover and then hesitate to tell anybody about. It's anything other than fancy, but it's full of special touches.

The grounds, about a fifteen-minute walk from town, are spacious

Olde Yard Inn, Virgin Gorda

and rambling with tropical flora and untamed paths. The main building contains a few guestrooms as well as the guest lounge, bar, and dining room. The guests congregate here at all times under the high, banana-thatched ceiling on comfortable orange- and yellow-cushioned couches fronted by backgammon games. The bar here serves all the usual tropical concoctions. The dining room adjoins, offering all three meals. The intimate dining spot with batik and bougainvillea decorations serves renowned French and Caribbean cuisine. Daily choices include home-made soups or pâté, escargots or coquilles, local fish or lobster, and their own seafood specialties.

The fourteen guestrooms are located in the main building as well as in a two-story structure to the rear. The guestrooms are all simply decorated and boast interesting pictures, colorful bedspreads, and private baths. A few of the rooms come with balcony, and one unit offers a four-poster bed for the romantics.

On the grounds, there is also a library, located in two octagonal buildings with wooden decks. Considered a focal point of the inn, the library offers an inviting area for reading, playing, or just relaxing.

Fellow guests form the entertainment at this quiet inn, making it a good hideaway for those wanting to retreat to good company.

Though not right on the water, the beach is a healthy fifteen-minute walk away.

✳

Also on the Island

Biras Creek Hotel
P.O. Box 54, Virgin Gorda, British Virgin Islands

Phone: (809) 494–3555

An away-from-it-all feeling combined with naturally good looks and good taste make Biras Creek an ideal retreat for those seeking barefoot seclusion.

This exclusive and quiet resort features more than 150 private acres with the thirty-two guest accommodations sprinkled carefully about. The resort offers luxury guestrooms as well as full facilities, including restaurant, beach, bar, swimming pool, tennis, and all water activities. The stay at Biras Creek includes breakfast, lunch, and dinner in the deluxe price range. Children under five cannot be accommodated.

Bitter End Yacht Club
P.O. Box 46, Virgin Gorda, British Virgin Islands

Phone: (809) 494–2746

The big focus here is sailing, as it is all over the Virgin Islands. Bitter End is indeed at the bitter end of Virgin Gorda, surrounded by water the color of green apples.

The elegantly furnished villas, ninety-eight in all, are perched on the hillside of this yachting resort; all boast views of the water. This yachting club spot offers unlimited use of the sixty-five sailboat fleet owned by the hotel, as well as snorkeling, scuba, and windsurfing.

Little Dix Bay
P.O. Box 70, Virgin Gorda, British Virgin Islands

Phone: (809) 495–5555
Reservations: Rockresorts Reservations

This Rockresort lives up to its reputation for natural beauty and modern comforts. Located walking distance from town, the 500-acre landscaped grounds are dotted with private guest bungalows, cacti, boulders, and pretty gardens. The beach at the hotel is secluded and protected, providing delightful air mattress lounging in crystal-clear water. The hotel offers full facilities, including restaurant, bar, tennis, all water sports, and horseback riding. Meals are unfailingly good with lots of fish (fresh out of the water), innovative salads, and impossible-to-skip desserts.

✳

Other Islands

Drake's Anchorage Resort Inn
Mosquito Island, British Virgin Islands
Mailing address: P.O. Box 2510, Virgin Gorda,
British Virgin Islands

Phone: (809) 494–2254; (800) 624–6651; or (617) 661–4745

Located in the North Sound, on an island of its own, this inn has just ten rooms (including two suites) in cottages perched on stilts along the shore. All the rooms are breezy and tropical, with rattan and wicker furniture and cool tile floors. There's a main lodge with a highly-regarded restaurant. Days are spent snorkeling, swimming, sailing, strolling along nature trails, and lolling around the island's beaches.

✳

Guana Island Club
Guana Island, British Virgin Islands

Phone: (809) 494–2354; (800) 544–8262; or (914) 967–6050

Off in a little island-world of its own, Guana Island plays host to no more than thirty guests at a time. Here the living couldn't be easier. Time is divided between swimming (with or without snorkel gear), hiking, birdwatching, sailing, and sunning. Accommodations are white-washed cottages simply decorated without televisions and radios.

✳

Peter Island Yacht Harbor and Hotel
P.O. Box 211, British Virgin Islands

Phone: (809) 494–2561; (800) 346–4451; or (616) 776–6456.

Arriving on this island is a little like visiting a country club. Everyone looks well-scrubbed and tanned and is either carrying a tennis racket or a tube of sun block. The most popular rooms are the beach villas, where you can have your own terrace overlooking the sea and a bathtub that opens up to a window garden.

※

Necker Island
Necker Island, British Virgin Islands
Mailing address: P.O. Box 315, Road Town, Tortola, British Virgin Islands

Phone: (809) 494–2757; (800) 225–4255; or (212) 696–4566
Representative: Resorts Management, Inc.

If you want a Caribbean island you can call your own, this is it. The entire 75-acre island (complete with a ten-bedroom Balinese-style villa) is "rented" out to parties of one to twenty people. The island is surrounded by a coral reef and white-sand beaches. Diversions include boating, tennis, hiking, and all-out relaxing.

British Leeward Islands

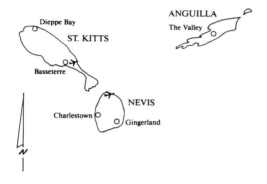

Dieppe Bay

ST. KITTS

Basseterre

ANGUILLA

The Valley

St. John's

ANTIGUA

English Harbour

NEVIS

Charlestown

Gingerland

N

MONTSERRAT

Plymouth

*L*ocated between Guadeloupe and the U.S. Virgin Islands are the British Leeward Islands, boasting sugar-white beaches and "island-hopping" proximity to each other. Antigua and perhaps St. Kitts were the major tourism islands here until relatively recently, when visitors began to discover the charms of "Irish" Montserrat, mountainous Nevis, and the eel-shaped little island of Anguilla. The money system on all of the British Leeward Islands is the Eastern Caribbean dollar (EC$), although U.S. dollars are often accepted as well. The British Leeward Islands are in the Atlantic Standard Time zone except during Daylight Saving season when the time on these islands is the same as Eastern Daylight Time.

Antigua

Antigua and its sixty-two-square-mile neighbor island thirty miles away, Barbuda, share a common history of British Colonial rule and today make up an independent nation administered by a Prime Minister and Upper and Lower Houses. Their combined population is around 70,000, with 30,000 in the capital city of St. John's, Antigua.

Cooling trade winds and a lower humidity level keep both islands pleasant year-round, with temperatures usually fluctuating between 71 and 86 degrees. Antigua, 108 miles square, is characterized by gently rolling hills and pastoral fields not dissimilar to the California countryside, with highlands rising to 1,330 feet and a rain forest region that is perpetually green. Barbuda, a coral island, is low, with tall shrubs and trees and little rainfall.

Antigua has one international airport, modern and well kept, that is served by several major airlines and many local carriers. Antigua is a favorite port-of-call for cruise liners. Both islands are just minutes away by air from the rest of the British Leeward Islands.

Both Antigua and Barbuda are surrounded by protective reefs and miles of sandy, conch-filled beaches, the color pink in Barbuda. Off the coast of Barbuda are many famous shipwrecks; exploring them is a favorite with divers. Visitors to Barbuda also enjoy the Frigate Bird Sanctuary and The Caves, a chance to explore fascinating underwater caves. Antigua's dry climate and topography make sports plentiful. The visitor will see many cricket fields (the national sport), two excellent golf courses, and water activities, including scuba diving, waterskiing, windsurfing, parasailing, and deep-sea fishing. Tennis enthusiasts are treated to two professional tournaments in January each year. Carnival takes place the end of July with lots of local color and flowing rum. The last week of April is "Sailing Week," featuring yacht races and more parties and rum. Several rental cars and taxis are available for touring, whether it be for sport, enjoying the clear blue-green water, or maybe just counting sugar mills. When renting a car, take into consideration that the roads are bumpy and slower than you might anticipate. Also, the roads are not always well-signed, but the friendly local people who happily offer directions more than make up for that deficiency.

Many local artists produce crafts in Antigua. A popular handicraft is the Warri Board, made for a seed game originally from Africa. A visit to the Seaview Farm and its potters is interesting.

Antigua is quite small, so it's possible to see the customary sights in about a day and a half and spend the rest of the time perfecting your backhand or improving your tan.

If you're not big on sightseeing, at least visit Nelson's Dockyard, a restoration project on the waterfront in English Harbour. From 1707 to 1899 the harbor was the main British naval base in the West Indies, at one point commanded by none other than Admiral Horatio Nelson. Thanks to the Friends of English Harbour, a British nonprofit organization, and its successors, several of the buildings have been fastidiously restored, making the dockyard the island's most celebrated attraction.

The main buildings in the yard are the Admiral's House, which was built in 1855 and now houses a museum; the Copper and Lumber Store, built in 1782; and the Admiral's Inn, constructed of brick brought from England as ship's ballast 200 years ago.

Just north of Nelson's Dockyard lies Shirley Heights, a ridge of extensive fortifications now largely in ruin, where you can get a terrific fort's view of the island.

The best time to visit St. John's, the island's capital and only real city, is early Saturday morning, when local farmers come to sell the week's crop. Other highlights in town include the enormous Cathedral of St. John the Divine, Redcliffe Quay (a row of restored buildings that once housed slaves prior to auction and now a collection of boutiques and restaurants), and the Museum of Antigua and Barbuda.

Antigua's most beautiful scenery is visible from Fig Tree Drive, which winds over the island's hilliest landscape, through a dense green rain forest, and along a Tahitiesque coastline of sun-baked fishing villages and white-sand beaches.

Nightlife on the islands is limited to hotel offerings that are often colorful shows with limbo dancers, calypso, and fire-eaters. The development of luxury hotels and condominium complexes to meet the increasing tourism needs of the island has brought a casino and many fine restaurants to Antigua. A common local food served there is black pudding, a well-seasoned dish made of intestines and rice. Antigua is also famous for its very sweet pineapples grown in black sand.

For more information on Antigua and Barbuda contact:

Antigua and Barbuda Department of Tourism
610 Fifth Avenue, Suite 311
New York, NY 10020
(212) 541–4117

＊

The Admiral's Inn
Nelson's Dockyard, English Harbour, P.O. Box 731, St. John's, Antigua, West Indies

Phone: (809) 463–1027
Representative: American Wolfe International
Key: Historic inn; 14 units; Moderate/Inexpensive EP; AE, MC, VI.
Location: ¹/₂ mi. to beach; 12 mi. to town; 14 mi. to airport.

Situated right at the entrance to the historic Nelson's Dockyard complex, Admiral's Inn is composed of two 1799 former offices and storage buildings of the old naval service center. The weathered brick buildings with blue shutters and white French doors boast their own waterfront terrace and lawn areas on this quiet corner of the dockyard.

The high-ceilinged structures have original beam ceilings and the old stonework walls. The lounge is decorated in comfortable seating with tropical-printed rattan sofas and chairs, a cozy bar, and captain's chairs on the adjacent terrace overlooking the lawn and harbor.

The fourteen guestrooms at the "nautical" inn are all different and decorated simply but comfortably in period style with twin beds, fans or air conditioners, and private baths with showers. One of the guestrooms features a pretty four-poster bed with canopy.

If the guest wishes, dinner and breakfast may be included for an additional rate; the menu is varied with several choices at each meal. Luncheon is served on the terrace or a box lunch may be offered for a day of beach-going or sailing. Steel bands play at the inn each Saturday night and sometimes local bands provide dancing in this informal atmosphere.

Ethelyn Phillip has been the congenial manager of the Admiral's

The Admiral's Inn, Antigua

Inn for many of its thirty years in operation and will personally see to it that your stay is relaxing and comfortable.

Note: The inn is closed the month of September and in early October.

✳

The Copper and Lumber Store
Nelson's Dockyard, English Harbour, P.O. Box 184, St. John's, Antigua, West Indies

Phone: (809) 460–1058; (800) 633–7411
Key: Historic inn; 14 units; Deluxe/Deluxe AP; AE, VI, MC.
Location: ¹/₂ mi. to beach; 12 mi. to town; 14 mi. to airport.

The Copper and Lumber Store is more than a beautifully restored inn—it is a slice of maritime history that has become a glorious addition to the Nelson's Dockyard complex of various dockyard buildings from the eighteenth-century.

The beautiful old brick building with steel-blue shutters and distinctive symmetrical, curved protrusions has an ornately carved ship's lady over the doorway, a reminder of its origins. A stately palm in front of the inn has a plaque that reads "planted by her majesty Queen Eliza-

The Copper and Lumber Store, Antigua

beth II 20 February 1966." The guest enters through a small reception area into the guest lounge filled with Oriental rugs, antique leather couches, and formal chairs—all contrasted warmly against the old exposed-brick walls. Antique dining tables and chairs, a freelance bar built into a brick archway, restored wood columns, and wonderful old wooden beams further enhance this both comfortable and elegant living room area. Every detail is authentic here, and throughout the inn old map prints, silver and copper decorative pieces, and beautiful brass lamps are apparent.

Upstairs are the fourteen guestrooms, all situated around the lovely courtyard. All of the guestrooms are suites and boast fully equipped kitchens and full maid service. The one-bedroom suites have a spacious living room area with day beds or a queen-size sleeper-couch. But, beyond these similarities, you will find very little the same in each of the authentically and individually decorated units. Furnishings, which are a combination of antiques and reproductions, are of eighteenth-century style and include many four-posters and unusual pieces. Marvelous wooden floors, some with stenciled borders, antique-patterned wallcoverings, baths with brass fixtures and mahogany-lined showers, fancy scrolled wooden banisters in split-level units, and decorating details such as brass lamps, old china, coordinated fabric prints and Williamsburg design bedspreads, fresh plants, Oriental carpets, and authentic wall prints fill each unit with the past.

Some of the units have dormer windows overlooking the harbor, and all open to the balcony overlooking the courtyard. There is also a restaurant that looks out on the courtyard.

✸

Also on the Island

Curtain Bluff
P.O. Box 288, Antigua, West Indies

Phone: (809) 462–8400; (212) 289–8888

Built into a hill with achingly beautiful views of the sea, Curtain Bluff is one of the island's most elegant hotels. All the rooms face the water and have private balconies or lanais, cool tile floors, and white wicker furnishings. Sports activities include snorkeling, sailing, tennis, and golf. There are two beaches right on the property, including one windward and one leeward.

The Inn at English Harbour
P.O. Box 187, St. John's, Antigua, West Indies

Phone: (809) 463–1014

This medium-sized inn at the entrance to historic English Harbour offers twenty-eight guestrooms and suites in two-story buildings near the sand. The mainly beachfront accommodations on pretty Freeman's Bay are attractively decorated with contemporary furniture, including lots of wicker. Each one has a patio or a balcony.

Jumby Bay Resort
P.O. Box 243, Long Island, Antigua, West Indies

Phone: (809) 462–6000; or (800) 421–9016

Jumby Bay is a marvelously exclusive resort poised on its own 300-acre island. Only a twelve-minute boat ride away from the mainland, this resort is completely self-sufficient. It offers an exhausting list of activities, including tennis, hiking, biking, croquet, and water sports from two beaches (one leeward, one windward). There's exceptional dining in the Estate House (continental cooking with an emphasis on fish), along with a handsome selection of rooms and suites. There are a total of 38 units, in octagonal-shaped cottages and the mission-style Pond Bay House. Tile floors, cotton rugs, and wicker furniture make for breezy luxury.

Long Bay Hotel
P.O. Box 442, St. John's, Antigua, West Indies

Phone: (809) 463–2005

This family-run hotel gives its guests, who return faithfully, special attention in its very private peninsula location. The twenty guestrooms are located in two-story buildings that are near the sheltered coral beach and boast private baths and comfortable, modern decor. Six cottages are also available. Long Bay Hotel has a country inn feel with chintz fabrics and wicker and offers guests a library and game room. The ¼-mile-long beach at Long Bay provides good snorkeling and scuba, and the inn offers a championship tennis court.

✴

St. Kitts and Nevis

The sister islands of St. Kitts and Nevis are the Caribbean in its pristine form . . . unspoiled, untamed, uncrowded. Here you find miles of untouched beach. You can stay in a lovely old plantation house and wake with the birds. You can sip ice tea with a sprig of mint on the veranda and take dips between chapters in a good novel. The two are situated in the northern part of the Leeward Islands and separated by a strait just two miles wide. They gained full political independence from Britain in September, 1983, and the 54,800 population is governed by a democratic form of government. The islands have an average temperature of 79 degrees, with northeast trade winds keeping the otherwise hot days quite pleasant.

Getting to St. Kitts and Nevis by air is achieved via connections with local Caribbean airlines that fly directly from other islands in the Caribbean. Because these islands are so small it is not difficult to get anywhere; taxis are available for tours as are comfortable sightseeing buses. The taxi drivers on St. Kitts attend classes on tourist information and are quite knowledgeable about the sights. They are also quite willing to take you to a destination and return at a requested time. Rental cars and cycles are available from several rental agencies, but a temporary license must be obtained. Driving is on the left side of the road. A forty-five minute ferry operates on a regular schedule between St. Kitts and Nevis for fairly easy island hopping. Wednesday is the favorite ferry-day for tourists when the schedule allows for an all-day visit to the sister island. Upon leaving the two islands a nominal departure tax is collected.

English is the principal language of the islands, but electrical current is not North American, requiring adapters in most of the lodgings. Shopping specialties on St. Kitts and Nevis include locally produced batik and tie-dye clothing and fabrics, homemade jellies and jams, and hand-embroidered items. The Romney Manor, located down a peaceful country road, is famous for its Caribelle Batik factory, but is most notable for its lovely gardens and picturesque, 350-year-old "rain tree."

For additional information on St. Kitts and Nevis contact:

St. Kitts-Nevis Tourist Board
414 E. 75th Street, 5th Floor
New York, NY 10001
(212) 535–1234

✳

St. Kitts

St. Kitts is the larger of the two islands and is made up of rich rolling sugar cane fields, rain forests with exotic birds and vegetation, pastoral scenes and golden and black sand beaches in its sixty-five-mile-square area. The capital is Basseterre, an eighteenth-century British town with white colonial houses on palm-lined streets. People congregate at the town's active harbor; at the town square, Circus, with its tall green Victorian clock; and at Independence Mall (formerly called Pall Mall), the former slave market that is now a lovely square surrounded by large, Georgian-style homes. Fresh vegetables, fruit, and tropical flowers from the fields are brought to market there now.

Visitors to St. Kitts will also be interested in the Brimstone Hill

Fortress, a leftover from British and French battles over the island, with 360-degree views of the hills and ocean. Mt. Misery is the island's looming volcanic crater. There is talk of changing the name to Mount Limauiga, the original name given St. Kitts by the Carib Indians. A guided hike through the rain forest can be strenuous, but natural waterfalls and glimpses of the island's famous "Velvet Monkeys" make it well worthwhile.

The nightlife in St. Kitts consists of a few bars and discos as well as a gambling casino at the Royal St. Kitts Hotel. The hotels in St. Kitts sometimes organize brass and steel band and calypso shows. Restaurants specialize in West Indian and creole foods.

✸

Fairview Inn
P.O. Box 212, St. Kitts, West Indies

Phone: (809) 465–2472
Representative: International Travel and Resorts
Key: Historic inn; 30 units; Moderate/Inexpensive EP; AE, VI, MC, DS.
Location: ¹/₂ mi. to beach; 3 mi. to town; 5 mi. to airport.

This country inn and cottage complex climbs a knoll a few miles out of town and offers breathtaking views of the ocean and St. Kitt's sister island, Nevis. A French eighteenth-century great house, which may have been the residence of the commander of the French troops based in the area, is the traditional part of the lodging establishment, and the dozen cottages that have been added around the garden-filled grounds offer a more contemporary choice in lodging. The Fairview opened as the pioneer resort hotel of the island in 1969 under the skillful direction of owners and managers Fred and Betty Lam. The Lams converted the private residence into a quaint West Indian inn and restaurant and have earned the respect of many return guests, including some royalty.

The quiet inn with sugar fields in front and hills to the rear is filled with sweet smells of the ever-flowering gardens. The 1700 home with white wooden siding, shingled roof, and fancy trim sits up proudly from the manicured garden and features a long front brick-lined veranda. You first view the reception area, parlor, and dining room when entering the inn. Oriental rugs fill the polished wooden floors, and the vaulted ceiling bears pretty, carved beams and a brass chandelier. Only

Fairview Inn, St. Kitts

a pair of etched-glass doors separate the period rooms, which are decorated in antiques, stained glass, and plants. Three guestrooms are located in the home itself and are usually rented only when the cottages are full or on special request.

Although the cottage accommodations represent a more contemporary offering in age and furnishings, the Lams took great care to include a pleasant blending of the old in the design. The cottages, dotted around the hillside grounds in back of the main house, were built from old stone found on the property; many feature stained-glass windows over the doorways. Each of the units has a wood-beamed ceiling and a unique character. The cottages uniformly contain built-in closets, tile or carpeted floors, modern baths with shower stalls, and contemporary furnishings. Either air conditioning or fans are available, as well as twin or queen beds. Some of the units are suites containing a hide-a-bed in the living room area to sleep four comfortably, as well as a private patio. The cottage units are well spaced with lots of grassy area in between the flower-lined paths leading to each.

A sparkling blue pool surrounded by lounges and offering inspiring views of the ocean sits next to another grassy lawn with picturesque fountain to the side of the house. A terrace with white latticework, wrought-iron chairs, tables, and plants, along with the inn's bar, connects. Spacious guest baths by the pool area add a nice touch.

The West Indian cuisine at the Fairview has received many praises and features fruit and vegetables fresh out of the gardens of the inn.

The sea-view patio is the locale of most meals at the Fairview; these are served cheerfully by the friendly Kittitian staff.

※

Rawlins Plantation
P.O. Box 340, St. Kitts, West Indies

Phone: (809) 465–6221
Representative: Rawlins Plantation, Mass. and Jacques de Larsay
Key: Plantation; 10 units; Deluxe/Deluxe MAP; No credit cards.
Location: Countryside; 1 mi. to beach; 14 mi. to airport.

You have to look carefully for the sign on the telephone pole that leads you up a long, winding dirt road through sugar cane fields to the plantation estate that sits atop a hill with masterful views of the fields below as well as the ocean in the distance. The drive sets the tone of the resort, a tranquil country inn that blends plantation history with homey accommodations.

The plantation's original home burned down several decades ago, but—thanks to the former owners, Philip and Frances Walwyn—new structures were built to mix carefully with the ruins on the estate grounds back in the early seventies. Today, an English country house contains the dining room and guest lounges of the inn; several cottages are widely spaced on the rolling, grassy acreage that surrounds. The main house, like the cottages, is constructed of white cement and has attractive yellow shutters and Victorian gingerbread trim and lattice-work. The old stone used on the buildings blends lovingly with the ruins that are found about in various stages of restoration.

The upstairs terrace of the main house has comfortable seating with inspiring views, and the connecting parlor boasts pretty wooden floors, a mixture of rattan and antique furnishings, a large library to fill the lazy hours here, and wide French doors. The adjacent dining room has an antique table and chair set, a large built-in bookcase, candles for elegant dinner settings, and a silver tea service. An outside terrace provides a less formal eating area with an arched stone wall entrance, white lattice, and white wrought-iron tables and chairs.

The cottages at the Rawlins Plantation resemble little houses and are beautifully private with lots of rolling lawn and tropical flowers in between. Most notable is the Windmill Suite, a tri-level unit built into

Rawlins Plantation, St. Kitts

the ruins of the plantation windmill. A white iron bed with canopy and a dressing table with old-fashioned skirting occupy the top level of the suite; the middle level is a large landing with baskets and china figurines, and the bottom of the suite consists of the living room with attractive French doors and bright flower prints. The bath has a clever, deep shower built into the curve of the windmill's old stone walls.

Recreation at the plantation includes a large tiled pool with gazebo overlooking the grassy fields and tennis courts below, as well as horseback riding and croquet.

The stay at Rawlins Plantation includes breakfast, dinner, and an afternoon tea, making the rate more reasonable that it might first appear. A buffet lunch or box lunch is also available so that you need never leave these peaceful grounds. The plantation's new owners/managers are Paul and Claire Rawson.

✳

Also on the Island

The Golden Lemon
Dieppe Bay Town, St. Kitts, West Indies

Phone: (809) 465–7260
Representative: Caribbean Inns Ltd.; Jacques de Larsay

117

The Golden Lemon, St. Kitts

Propped up on the shores of a black-sand beach amid long-trunk-ed palm trees stands The Golden Lemon, a legendary hotel on St. Kitts. Guests have a choice of accommodations: either those in the seventeenth-century French manor house, in its eighteenth-century addition, or in the contemporary seaside townhouses. Each room is beautiful enough to be on the pages of a glossy home furnishings magazine, and indeed, the owner—Arthur Leaman—was an editor at *House and Garden*. The Golden Lemon is a small, clubby property, with one-week minimum (and two-week maximum) stays. Rates are always deluxe, MAP. In addition to the beach (off of which there is a wonderful reef for snorkeling), a pool and a tennis court are available.

Ocean Terrace Inn
P.O. Box 65, Basseterre, St. Kitts, West Indies

Phone: (809) 465–2754 or 465–4121
Representative: American Wolfe International

Overlooking the bay of Basseterre is this hillside-terraced hotel that has grown from its original "small inn" status to hotel in recent years. The charm is still evident throughout the beautifully landscaped grounds with fountain, old-fashioned swing, flowing lawns, and antique cannons. The fifty-two units are nicely furnished with telephones and radios, air conditioning, patios or balconies, cable television, and some mini-refrigerators. Self-contained apartments are also available. The inn offers two fresh water swimming pools, an open-air Jacuzzi, bar, entertainment in the evenings, good Caribbean cuisine, and shops.

Ottley's Plantation Inn
P.O. Box 345, Basseterre, St. Kitts, West Indies

Phone: (809) 465–4760
Representative: Jacques de Larsay

Perched high on a hill, Ottley's is a 1706 great house-turned-inn. Its fifteen rooms (nine in the guesthouse and six in cottages) all have their own bathrooms, air-conditioning, and ceiling fans, balconies or lanais, and individual telephones. The big focus here is on the food, especially the Sunday Champagne brunch. Diversions include walking through Ottley's private rain forest and swimming—or just splashing about—in the enormous spring-fed pool. There are also beaches nearby and tennis, golf, horseback riding, and sailing can be easily arranged. MAP prices are deluxe year-round.

The White House
Box 436, St. Peter's, St. Kitts, West Indies

Phone: (809) 465–8162

Staying at The White House really feels like stepping back 250 years. In its earlier life, it was the home of a colonial plantation owner. Today, it is impeccably restored and offers ten guest rooms. All are tastefully decorated with Laura Ashley fabrics and polished antiques. There are no radios, televisions, or air conditioning (which is not necessary due to ceiling fans and thick walls). There's a swimming pool, a tennis court, and a croquet lawn. Prices are deluxe, MAP year round.

✳

Nevis

The island of Nevis was settled by the British in 1628 and in the eighteenth century became the "Queen of the Caribees" as the leading spa of the West Indies, due to its hot mineral springs. Sea island cotton is the principal crop today, but Nevis boasted prosperous sugar cane estates at one time. These estates of yesterday have been transformed into beautiful inns, many discussed in the listings that follow. Touring these fine, historic inns is also the main tourist activity on the small island.

Nevis is an island of unspoiled beauty with miles of white sandy beaches lined with palms. Some consider Pinney's Beach to be one of the best beaches in the Caribbean. A strenuous, but popular, hike 3,500 feet up Mt. Nevis to its extinct volcanic crater is an all-day event.

The capital of Nevis, Charlestown, is known for its distinctive houses built out of locally quarried volcanic stone. The ferry from St. Kitts docks right in the heart of the little town, and rental cars and taxis await just steps away. A rental car can be obtained, allowing for a leisurely all-day tour around the small island. The roads on Nevis are bumpy and curvy, but lined with lush tropical vegetation, pretty ocean vistas, and numerous sugar mill ruins.

※

Golden Rock Estate
Box 493, Gingerland, Nevis, West Indies

Phone: (809) 469–3346
Representative: International Travel & Resorts; Jacques de Larsay
Key: Plantation; 16 units; Expensive/Moderate EP; No credit cards.
Location: 1 mi. to beach; 3 mi. to town; 10 mi. to airport.

This former plantation is hidden from the road up a winding drive lined with tropical groves. The estate house, dating back to the early 1800s, is constructed of ancient stone and accented by pale yellow wooden shutters, arched doorways, and cascading bougainvillea. Inside, the guest lounge offers comfortable seating and an abundance of books amid the old stone floors and walls with low, yellow-beamed ceilings. A short flight up is a bar built into the stone with an adjacent

Golden Rock Estate, Nevis

billiard and games room. The unusual gameroom ceiling has a fishing net that holds untamed ivy instead of the usual nautical touches. Another step up places you in the dining room with the same stone walls, an antique buffet and a silver tea service. Plants and ivy decorate the walls here and small baskets of fresh posies are centered on the blue tablecloths.

The hillside grounds of the inn are dotted with cottages that provide guest accommodations, the Sugar Mill suite, an inviting pool, tennis courts, and rambling tropical gardens full of the sounds and sweet smells of the rural countryside. For a slight additional fee and on arrangement only, the Sugar Mill suite, the 1811 renovated mill of the plantation, can be reserved for up to four or five people, although it is a favorite honeymooner's retreat. This duplex features double four-poster beds with canopies downstairs and a massive king-size canopy bed upstairs with intricate, antique carvings. The staircase of the mill cures with the turn of the old stone walls. The remainder of the guest accommodations, located in cottages about the grounds, offer attractive furnishings such as custom bamboo four-poster beds and dressing rooms and private baths. Each unit is very private and provides a private patio where you may chose to breakfast in the morning.

On the grounds, there is a spring-fed pool and a tennis court; nearby is the inn's private eleven-acre beach property where guests can snorkel and windsurf for free (transportation is arranged).

Owner Pam Barry (a descendant of the original plantation family) is known for her hospitable nature.

❋

Montpelier Plantation Inn
Charlestown, P.O. Box 474, Nevis, West Indies

Phone: (809) 469-3462
Representative: Ray Morrow Associates; Jacques de Larsay
Key: Plantation; 16 units; Deluxe/Deluxe MAP; No credit cards.
Location: 3 mi. to beach; 2 mi. to town; 10 mi. to airport.

The Montpelier Plantation is nicely tucked away down what might be called a residential lane by local people, but a rural country road with ruts and chickens to anyone else. Once you get there, you are glad it is hidden, in hopes not many others will discover its charming attributes and turn it into a less personal retreat. The gracious owners, James and Celia Milnes Gaskell, will probably not let such a thing happen anyway because it is obviously their home as well; you feel that special, homestyle touch in every detail at Montpelier.

Eight guest bungalows are scattered on the vast grounds of the plantation along with the attractive West Indian great house, a pool, bar, dining area, and the plantation's exceptional organic gardens—the pride of its owners. The plantation's organic farm and orchards, along with its fishing boat, supply the basis of the delicious homemade, natural cuisine of the inn.

A large swimming pool at the plantation retains an impressive mural with Nevis scenery on the privacy wall and blends well with the surrounding tropical vegetation. Overlooking the pool is a semi-enclosed bar with attractive rattan seating covered in a blue and rust tropical print. A few steps up lead to the dining room, facing a handsome mill ruin, with a stone planter in the middle, walls with colorful murals, and white tablecloths set in pretty blue and white china. The patio surrounding the dining room is a tranquil luncheon spot where a generous buffet is offered among the stone arches dripping with plants.

The great house, framed in front by an ancient weeping fig tree, has an English country house look, featuring large rooms with polished wood-inlaid floors, domed ceilings, French doors, and arched-stone entries. The furnishings are warm and elegant, boasting antique tables,

Montpelier Plantation Inn, Nevis

old portraits, a hoosier with china, and coordinated orange chintz sofas and draperies. Plants bring the peaceful outside in, and a large veranda on one side provides intimate nighttime dining. The parlor also contains the nighttime bar and is the gathering spot after the sun goes down.

The pastel stucco bungalows housing guests are scattered along a winding path with manicured lawns in between. The bungalows contain two units each and are decorated attractively in comfortable rattan furnishings with pretty print draperies. Each one has a private patio and view of the ocean.

In addition to the pool, a tennis court surrounded by coconut trees is located on the spacious grounds, and the Gaskells provide free transportation to the nearby beaches.

Both breakfast and dinner are included in the stay at Montpelier and lunch is available. The full breakfast fare includes tropical fruits, a main course, and homemade bread and marmalade; dinner is table d'hote with three courses brimming with fresh, local ingredients. The food at the inn, which can be described as sublime, is made from whole wheat flours; all that can be is homemade. The coconut cream pie is a real specialty.

For a true "home away from home" experience on this quiet little island, the Montpelier never fails to provide a personalized getaway for its special guests.

✳

Nisbet Plantation Inn
Nevis, West Indies

Phone: (809) 469–9325; (800) 344–2049
Key: Plantation; 38 units; Deluxe/Deluxe MAP; AE, MC, VI.
Location: On beach; 8 mi. to town; 1 mi. to airport.

Although no one could quibble that the Nisbet Plantation presents a beautiful picture from the front, there are few plantation scenes that can surpass the Nisbet's view from its upper-back terrace. On this pretty outdoor patio, guests may dine on quaint burgundy-printed china and gaze at the sweeping vista of the ocean 500 yards ahead through a perfectly placed path lined with giant coconut palms. If you dare turn your eyes from the tree-lined focus, you'll also take in the well-manicured grassy grounds, tropical gardens, tennis courts, and the various cottages that house the small group of guests at the plantation.

The Nisbet Plantation is nicely situated on a pretty half-mile beach on grounds spacious enough that you might want to request a cottage either near the beach or near the main house. A walk in either direction is a pleasant, tranquil stroll. The inn was built on the site of an eighteenth-century sugar plantation; some of the historic ruins, with tropical vegetation pushing out of the cracks and crevices, are visible in the curve of the front circular drive. The Great House itself was rebuilt around the turn of the century and has fancy gingerbread trim, coral stonework, white shutters and a second-story, screened-in sunporch reminiscent of those graceful days.

The guest parlor and dining room of the house feature antique furnishings, country chintz fabrics, and comfort. The dining room has walls of gathered pink material and subtle wallcoverings in the same old-fashioned theme. The tables of the formal dining area are punctuated with small china vases filled with petite flower arrangements; a built-in shelf displays antique china and glassware. The attractive wooden floors are bare except for an occasional straw mat. The sunporch and connecting bar at the inn add a more casual touch and are decorated in a mixture of antiques and island furnishings of bamboo and rattan. There is also a library in this area.

The nineteen cottages of the inn are sprinkled about the thirty-acre grounds, granting maximum privacy and solitude. Most of the cottages house two guest facilities, and each guestroom is named after an old plantation on Nevis. Most of the cottages are more contemporary

Nisbet Plantation Inn, Nevis

than the main house, while the more interesting appear about the same vintage. The later-built cottages are attractively designed with vaulted ceilings, walk-in closets, modern baths with large shower stalls, and views of the ocean, and are furnished in rattan, pretty fabrics, and some antiques. The older cottages have the same fancy gingerbread, white frame and lattice construction as the Great House and details such as French doors with matching shutters. The "Gingerland" is a favorite at the Nisbet and features two ornately carved, twin canopy beds with patchwork quilt spreads. But not to forego comfort, the bath is quite modern.

The on-season and off-season stay at Nisbet includes both breakfast and dinner, with complimentary wine served with the evening meal. Breakfast is served in the Great House, in the guest's room, or on the beach. Afternoon tea, cocktails, and dinner are offered in the Great House, allowing guests to get acquainted in their elegant yet intimate surroundings. A beachfront restaurant and bar at Nisbet also offers lunch as well as dreamy moonlight barbecues. A boutique on the plantation sells island handicrafts and necessities.

✳

Croney's Old Manor Estate
P.O. Box 70, Charlestown, Nevis, West Indies

Phone: (809) 465–5445
Key: Plantation; 10 units; Expensive/Expensive EP; AE, MC, VI.
Location: 1 mi. to beach; 3 mi. to town; 10 mi. to airport.

This small plantation-inn is appropriately named, since a first impression of the secluded establishment is of an exclusive estate. Croney was a former estate owner. The restored plantation dates back to a 1690 land grant; several of the stone-constructed buildings were built in the late 1700s through 1832.

The Cooperage Dining Room is a separate building where barrels for the sugar mill were once made. The eating spot now holds rattan tables and chairs and a pleasant veranda connects with views of the sea. The garden, with ruins of the kitchen stone hearth, is a favorite locale for lunch and the Friday night steak and lobster buffet.

The guestrooms at the plantation are located in restored buildings around the Sugar Mill and the great house. The attractive furnishings in guestrooms and suites include king size or twin canopy beds and modern conveniences.

The staff at the Old Manor Estate provides free beach and town transportation and welcomes the guest with a drink. A picturesque freshwater pool is nestled within the lush, tropical grounds in this most relaxing and intimate spot.

✳

Also on the Island

Hermitage Plantation
Nevis, West Indies

Phone: (809) 469–3477
Representative: International Travel & Resorts, Inc.; Robert Reid Associates

This hilltopping plantation is home to the oldest occupied house in the Antilles. There are a dozen guest rooms in the restored Carriage House and newer garden villas. All are attractively furnished with four-poster canopy beds and antique pieces. Each room has its own hammock on a porch facing the sea. A pool and shuttle van to the beach are available. Rates are Deluxe/Moderate MAP.

✺

Montserrat

Montserrat, twelve miles long and seven miles wide, is located some twenty-seven miles from Antigua. The lush green mountainous scenery, traversed by numerous rivers and streams, is often compared to Ireland, and the little island has adopted the shamrock as a symbol of these similarities. Actually, the first European settlers in 1632 were Catholic-Irish fleeing from religious persecution, and these settlers left evidence of their existence in the island's various place names.

English is the spoken language on the island. The current population is about 12,000 in this British Dependent Territory with a resident Governor appointed by the Queen. Montserrat is reached through connection in Antigua, the closest international airport, which offers several fifteen-minute flights daily. The electrical current does require a transformer for U.S. appliances.

Plymouth, the island's capital, has a population of about 4,000 and boasts many fine Georgian houses. The Post Office and Treasury, located in a lovely colonial structure, produces the beautiful postage stamps after by collectors.

Fine tennis and golf are available, as well as nature trails that lead hikers by waterfalls to the steaming center of the island's volcano. History can be relived by exploring the ruins of an old rum distillery in the highlands or by visiting the island's museum, housed in an old restored sugar mill. Beachgoers will enjoy Montserrat's unusual black sands.

The local specialties on Montserrat range from roasted fresh coconut chips, called *hospitality chips,* to beautiful handcrafted tapestries made of yarn, cotton, or linen.

For more information on Montserrat contact:

Caribbean Tourism Organization
20 East 46th Street
New York, NY 10017
(212) 682–0435

✺

Montserrat Springs Hotel
P.O. Box 259, Sturge Park Road, Plymouth, Montserrat, West Indies

Phone: (809) 491–2481 or 491–2482
Key: Inn; 46 units; Expensive/Moderate EP; VI, AE, MC.
Location: 200 yards to beach; 1 mi. to town; 9 mi. to airport.

Although the main buildings of Montserrat Springs were built in 1954, the entire hotel was renovated in 1987. Today, there are forty-six rooms (including six suites) located in a wing of the main building and in cottages along a hillside. All have private balconies, phones, and televisions.

Much of the activity here is centered around the picturesque swimming pool, as well as the hot mineral springs pool and Jacuzzi that overlook the water. There are also a beach and two tennis courts.

An open-air dining area with bar is the locale of all three meals, served from an a la carte menu with both international and Caribbean specialties. Special barbecues and entertainment highlight meals during on-season.

✻

Also on the Island

Vue Pointe
Olde Towne, Montserrat, West Indies

Phone: (809) 491–5210; (800) 223–6510

Vue Pointe is the kind of hotel guests return to year after year. Its accommodations are in individual rondavels, simply decorated and poised on a hillside above the sea. There is a main lodge with a bar, lounge area, terrace, and dining room. There are two tennis courts with lights, plus a water sports facility on the beach, a pool, and a golf course nearby. Rates are Expensive/Moderate EP.

✻

Anguilla

Anguilla is wonderful for what it doesn't have. There are no high-rise buildings, no flashy casinos, no cities.

Surrounded by white beaches and turquoise waters, the eel-shaped island of Anguilla is often referred to as "the best-kept secret island paradise in the world." Located on the northern tip of the Leeward chain, the sixteen-mile-long by four-mile-wide island is almost flat and treeless. The highest point is Crocus Hill, with a 213-foot elevation. Its surrounding waters reveal several offshore cays and coral reefs.

Anguilla is a British Colony with a population of about 7,000 of mainly African descent, but with European, especially Irish, influences. The monetary system is the Eastern Caribbean dollar, but U.S. money is widely accepted. Electrical voltage is compatible with U.S. appliances.

The nearest major airports to Anguilla are in St. Maarten, Antigua, St. Kitts, St. Thomas, and Puerto Rico; all offer direct, regularly scheduled flights to Anguilla. An efficient ferry system operates between St. Maarten and Anguilla daily, docking at Anguilla's Blowing Point Harbor. The trip takes just thirty-five minutes. Visitors to the island are required to have a valid passport and must pay a departure tax upon leaving. The roads in Anguilla are good, and driving is probably the best way to really explore the island. Vehicles travel on the left.

The beaches on Anguilla, some thirty in all, are immaculately clean, with white coral sand and hidden coves and grottos. Crescent-shaped Rendezvous Bay is a beautiful sunbathing and shell-collecting beach. Charter boats with fishing, scuba, or snorkeling equipment are available at several spots. Lobster diving is an integral part of the local economy, and abundant tropical fish may be viewed or spearfished.

Sights to see around the island include the Salt Ponds, two currently harvested salt lakes; the Irish fishing village of Island Harbour; the Fountain, a huge underwater cave of fresh water; and the Ruins of Dutch Fort, the scene of the 1796 French invasion of Anguilla. A few true desert islands are in close proximity to Anguilla and are reached by charter fishing boats or power boats. The main town on the island, The Village, is a settlement near Crocus Bay, where the French landed in the eighteenth-century.

The main industry of Anguilla is building boats, which are richly colored and designed for speed. Not surprisingly, the national sport is boat racing, with races held almost every holiday.

The entertainment on the island is limited to small bands at the hotels or restaurants. Island cuisine features freshly caught seafood and fish (red snapper a favorite), often cooked creole-style. Beach barbecue pits are set up to feed beach-goers a fish snack or even to cook the latest catch fresh off the boat while you wait.

For more information on Anguilla contact:
Anguilla Tourist Information
c/o Medhurst & Associates
271 Main Street
Northport, NY 11768
(516) 261–9600

✴

Cap Juluca
P.O. Box 240, Anguilla, British West Indies

Phone: (809) 497–6666; (800) 323–0139
Representative: Flagship Hotels & Resorts
Key: Inn; 48 units; Deluxe/Deluxe EP; AE.
Location: On the leeward coast, about fifteen minutes by taxi from the airport and ferry dock.

One of Anguilla's newest properties (opened about five years ago), Cap Juluca is a dazzling Moorish-style hotel on Maunday's Bay. It's about as luxurious as Caribbean hotels get, with guestrooms grandly furnished with enormous beds on raised platforms, lavish marble bathrooms that open onto private walled gardens, and separate dressing rooms. Some have kitchenettes. The centerpiece of the hotel is Pimms, the restaurant that sits open-air on the water's edge. There are two mile-long beaches (with an array of water sports) and three tennis courts with lights for night play.

✴

Cinnamon Reef Beach Club
Little Harbour, Anguilla, British West Indies

Phone: (809) 497–2727
Representative: Ralph Locke Islands
Key: Inn; 22 units; Deluxe/Moderate EP; AE, MC, VI.

With all the glamorous new West End hotels, it might be surprising that a non-glitzy property such as the Cinnamon Reef Beach Club would remain such a favorite. Nevertheless, it does. It's set on a little beach at Little Harbour that is ideal for sailing, windsurfing, and snorkeling. Rooms—which are actually suites—are all in individual bungalows with high ceilings and private patios. There's a main clubhouse where guests gather for meals (mostly seafood) with entertainment (local bands perform most evenings). There are a pool, three tennis courts, and a Jacuzzi.

*

Coccoloba
P.O. Box 332, Barnes Bay, Anguilla,
British West Indies

Phone: (809) 497–6871; (800) 833–3559
Key: Inn; 51 units; Deluxe/Deluxe CP; AE, MC, VI.
Location: On the water, between Barnes Bay and Meads Bay; twenty minutes from the ferry and airport.

Utterly devoted to the simple by-the-sea life, Coccoloba is the kind of place you fall in love with and then hesitate to tell anybody about

Coccoloba, Anguilla

131

for fear of it becoming too popular. There are fifty-one rooms, two of which are suites, in beachside cottages and a villa. Each one has a view of the sea and a private patio and is well-equipped with thoughtful touches (bathrobes, stocked refrigerators, hair dryers, walking canes, and umbrellas). The hotel's restaurant is outstanding, with a wonderful selection of seafood (and other) dishes competing for your attention. Manager Martin Flaherty is always on hand to take care of any little details, as well as liven up the party with his natural good cheer.

✳

Malliouhana
P.O. Box 173, Anguilla, British West Indies

Phone: (809) 497–6111
Representative: David B. Mitchell & Company, Inc.
Key: Inn; 52 units; Deluxe/Deluxe EP; No credit cards.
Location: On the northeast shore of the island; about ten minutes by taxi from the airstrip and the ferry pier.

Beautifully situated on Mead's Bay, the Malliouhana (the Arawak name for Anguilla) started the boom of new hotels on Anguilla about eight years ago. This is a very elegant property, where well-heeled guests divide their time between the pools (there are two), the tennis courts (four with lights), the exercise room (Nautilus equipment), the beach, and the water (for sailing, windsurfing, and water-skiing). There are thirty-four rooms plus eighteen one- or two-bedroom suites in the main building and in villas overlooking the beach or garden. Each one has a ceiling fan, a balcony or lanai, and mini-bar.

Dutch Windward Islands

ST. MAARTEN

Philipsburg

SABA Windwardside

The Bottom

ST. EUSTATIUS

N

*O*n his second voyage to the West Indies, Columbus was said to have sighted this lovely group of islands on the name day of San Martino (St. Martin of Tours). The largest island, surrounded by sparkling white beaches, then became known as Sint Maarten or Saint Martin, depending upon the Dutch or French point of view. After changing hands sixteen times, the island of Sint Maarten has held two peacefully coexisting nations for three centuries.

The three Windward islands of St. Maarten, Saba, and St. Eustatius (Statia), combined with Bonaire and Curacao, form the Netherlands Antilles islands of the Caribbean. The five islands are governed by a representative of the Queen of the Netherlands, and a parliamentary democracy allows each island territory a representative in the Island Council.

Regularly scheduled flights from North America into the Dutch Windward Islands, as well as from other Caribbean islands, are available, and cruise ships make frequent stops in St. Maarten. Day sails and charters out of Philipsburg to St. Barts, and small plane flights to Saba and Statia make island-hopping possible. A valid passport, birth certificate, or voter's registration card will admit U.S. citizens to the islands, and a nominal departure tax for persons over two years of age is collected upon leaving.

The official language of the Dutch Windwards is Dutch, but English is spoken widely and used on local television and radio programming. The currency is the NA florin or guilder. Both traveler's checks and credit cards, as well as the American dollar, are accepted in most establishments, but it is wise to check ahead. The electrical power is compatible with North American appliances. Getting around the islands is easy with both rental cars and taxis available, and traffic moves to the right. The island is on Atlantic Standard Time (one hour ahead of Eastern Standard Time) all year. During Daylight Saving season, the time on St. Maarten and in the Eastern U.S. is the same.

For further information on the Dutch Windward Islands contact:

Saba/St. Eustatius Tourist Office c/o Medhurst & Associates, Inc.
271 Main Street
Northport, NY 11768
(800) 344–4606; (212) 936–0050
or
St. Maarten Tourist Information Office
275 Seventh Avenue, 19th floor
New York, NY 10001
(212) 989–0000

✳

Saba

Just fifteen minutes by air from St. Maarten is this five-mile-square "unspoilt Queen of the Caribbean." Lushly green Saba is made up of four villages—The Bottom, Windwardside, St. John's, and Hell's Gate—that are connected by a single cross-island road full of hairpin turns through the mountains and ravines. Before the road, the villages on this volcanic cone-shaped island were united only by hundreds of steps chiseled by the 1640 Dutch settlers. Unlike most of the Caribbean islands, Saba has no real beaches; its surrounding rugged cliffs meet the sea below.

A trip through Saba, perhaps to the highest point at Mt. Scenery (2900 feet), can be made by taxi or on foot and is filled with breathtaking views and jagged rocks and boulders covered with orchids, lilies, and begonias. Along with nature's beauty are the charming villages of Saba, with their gingerbread-trimmed cottages clinging to the mountain sides, gabled roofs, and flower- and fern-filled gardens. Saba, really a mountain top, is cooler than the other Dutch Windward islands, averaging 78 degrees, with brief showers keeping the gardens and wild tropical flowers plentiful.

Saban women began their craft of intricate needlework when the men on the island took to the sea, although present-day Saban men are employed by the oil refineries of Aruba and Curacao. The Artisans Foundation promotes and sells silk-screened fabrics and clothing handmade by the Sabans; this has become an integral part of the local economy.

❋

Captain's Quarters
Windwardside, Saba, Netherlands Antilles

Phone: (011–599) 46–2201
Representative: International Travel & Resorts, Inc.; Jacques de Larsay
Key: Historic inn; 10 units; Moderate/Moderate CP; AE, MC, VI.
Location: Residential; Near town; 5 mi. to airport.

This early 1900s sea captain's home that forms the main house of the inn was built by Captain Henry Hassell for his daughter. It was used at one time in its history as a hospital, but opened as a charming turn-of-the-century lodging in 1965. Cuddled in the leeward slope of the village, this intimate group of three gingerbread houses with red tile roofs

Captain's Quarters, Saba

and Dutch blue shutters overlooks the sea 1,400 feet below.

The old sea captain's house, with its old-fashioned verandas, is now the office, library, and kitchen of the inn and holds a few of the guestrooms. The sitting room is furnished in a pleasant assortment of antiques and paintings. Adjoining the home is a shaded breakfast porch where guests may enjoy a full American fare in the tranquil surroundings. A few steps away is the arbored dining pavilion, a charming open-air patio decorated in rattan and Mexican trestle tables and surrounded and shaded by breadfruit and mango trees. This garden dining spot serves lunches and dinners of freshly caught lobster, grouper, and snapper, along with steak, veal, lamb, and other specialties.

A separate bar sits next to the inn's freshwater pool, which is surrounded by a spacious sunbathing deck on two sides and by aromatic trees and flowers; the ocean view from here is exceptional. Light lunches are also served in this scenic spot.

The guestrooms at the Captain's Quarters all boast modern, private baths and relaxing verandas or balconies with views of the tropical blooms that surround, the green hillsides, and the sparkling sea. These spacious rooms vary in size and decor, but all are furnished in a delightful mixture of mahogany antiques and island rattan and wicker. Romantic four-poster beds grace most of the accommodations.

Manager Joseph L. Johnson is on hand to provide guests with a truly relaxing stay among friends in this intimate and quaint inn.

✸

Cranston's Antique Inn
The Bottom, Saba, Netherlands Antilles

Phone: (011–599) 46–3203
Key: Historic inn; 6 units; Inexpensive CP year-round; No credit cards.
Location: In town; Near ocean; 5 mi. to airport.

This 1850-built inn in Saba's capital city has a congenial history of housing visitors. The 135-year-old frame structure that fronts the small roadway was a government guest house that regularly hosted Dutch officials, including Queen Juliana. For over forty years Mr. J. C. Cranston has been continuing the hospitality of the antique inn by offering six charming guest accommodations to island visitors.

The country inn is clean and cozy, decorated in a mixture of original house antiques and those collected by Mr. Cranston. The pretty hardwood floors add warmth, as do the printed curtains and bedspreads. Most notably, every guestroom hosts an impressive four-poster, the most formidable asset of each room. Queen Juliana's room is available to guests who want to relive history; it is on the second floor and boasts a tranquil garden view. Only one room at the inn has a private bath, and the remaining quarters adequately share two bathrooms.

This bed and breakfast offers the complimentary morning meal on the covered garden terrace, as well as lunches and dinners of tasty local food and vegetarian specialties.

Nestled between the green, volcanic hillsides of the island, Cranston's Antique Inn is within walking distance of the picturesque Ladder Bay, a network of over 500 steps leading to the coast.

✻

Scout's Place
Windwardside, Saba, Netherlands Antilles

Phone: (011–599) 46–2205
Key: Guest house; 15 units; Inexpensive EP year-round; MC, VI.
Location: In town; 3 mi. to harbor; 2 mi. to airport.

This 1920s-built guest house once housed government officials and passed through many hands until Scout Thirkield purchased the property and turned it into a modest, well-run lodging establishment.

Scout has sold the small inn to local Diana Medero, who is carrying on the guest house's reputation for congeniality most ably.

The old building, of Dutch architecture, holds a guest parlor with some Victorian furnishings and a color television. Five guestrooms are located here and feature some four-posters and antiques, as well as views of the flower-filled courtyard and the sea beyond. The homey accommodations include three rooms with private baths and two that share a bathroom. Ten new rooms are located in a newer addition. Each has a four-poster bed, reproduction antiques, a private bath, and a balcony.

This tranquil inn is right in the heart of things, in the center of town, and set gracefully on the ledge of a hill with its own pool. The staff is friendly and the pace is quiet.

＊

Also on the Island

Juliana's
Windwardside, Saba, Netherlands Antilles

Phone: (011–599) 46–2269

Juliana's is a small, meticulously run inn offering ten rooms plus a two-room apartment and a two-bedroom cottage. All are roomy and spotless and equipped with ceiling fans, clock/radios, and coffee makers. Each has a balcony. The cottage—called Flossie's Cottage—is full of West Indian charm (both inside and out) and has been the subject of many a watercolor, photograph, and oil painting. There are a pool and a restaurant—Tropics Cafe—serving breakfast and lunch only.

＊

St. Maarten

Thirty-seven-mile square St. Maarten, half Dutch and half French, is considered the smallest existing territory shared by two sovereign states. (See the "French West Indies" section for information about the French half.) The northernmost Antilles island, St. Maarten boasts a year-round average temperature of 80 degrees, with cooling trade winds, over thirty coral beaches, popular duty-free shopping, and active gambling casinos.

The capital of St. Maarten, Philipsburg, was founded in 1763 by

Commander Hohn Philips, a Scotsman in Dutch employ, and it is distinguished by unique shingled architecture. Philipsburg's shops line the two main thoroughfares, and little lanes called *steegjes* connect the streets with still more quaint stores. St. Maarten is a duty-free port with no local taxes imposed and some very reasonable rates on all kinds of merchandise, from designer jewelry and cameras to Holland cheeses. To the southwest of town are the ruins of seventeenth-century Fort Amsterdam, the first Dutch fort on the island.

St. Maarten's crystal-clear bays and coves offer superior snorkeling and scuba diving, with visibility of seventy-five to 125 feet. Deep-sea fishing charters for half or full day, coastal and lagoon cruises, and glass-bottomed boat trips are available for exploring the countless coves and bays around the island.

*

Mary's Boon
P.O. Box 2078, St. Maarten, Netherlands Antilles

Phone: (011–599) 55–4235; (800) 223–5608
Key: Inn; 12 units; Expensive/Moderate EP; No credit cards.
Location: On beach; 5 mi. to town; 2 mi. to Dutch airport.

The original owner of Mary's Boon, Caribbean innkeeper Mary Pomeroy, is the "Mary" in question, but the second half of the inn's name, meaning "welcome benefit," might be relevant to anyone who visits the intimate inn in search of a private stretch of beach and friendly surroundings. The small inn, located down a long private road on the snow-white sand of Juliana Beach, is now owned and managed by Rushton Little, who carries on the 1970-built inn's tradition of hospitality.

Mary's Boon is made up of gingerbread-adorned buildings and cottages with wooden balconies and verandas that boast elaborate hibiscus trim. The structures are situated directly on the sand, with gardens of shrubbery, sea grapes, and coconut palms growing in profusion. The desertion of this stretch of beach is interrupted only by an occasional plane landing or taking off from the airport runway that nearly touches the edge of the inn property. Even with that one inconvenience, the inn is still a favorite of a generous return clientele.

Guestrooms at Mary's Boon are really apartments; each is unique. The dozen spacious studios all boast private baths with tiled shower

Mary's Boon, St. Maarten

stalls and lots of fresh-air ventilation, tile floors, ceiling fans, kitch-enettes, and private seaside patios. The decor is light and airy, with lou-vered windows, beamed cathedral ceilings, Haitian paintings, and a nice combination of wicker, bamboo, and antique furnishings.

All three meals are served at the inn and offered in a pleasant open-air gallery with wood panelling and beamed ceiling. The bistro, with small tables and romantic nighttime lighting, fronts the pic-turesque bay. Guests at Mary's Boon enjoy a varied Dutch, French, and West Indian menu while gazing at the sparkling Caribbean a few feet ahead. A lounge area in the main building has a grand piano for infor-mal entertainment and comfortable, tropical seating.

✳

Pasanggrahan Royal Guest House

P.O. Box 151, 13 Front Street, Philipsburg, St. Maarten, Netherlands Antilles

Phone: (011–599) 52–3588
Representative: International Travel & Resorts, Inc.
Key: Historic inn; 32 units; Moderate/Moderate EP; VI, MC, AE.
Location: On beach; In town; 7 mi. to Dutch airport.

Pasanggrahan, an Indonesian word, means "the great house," and is a most appropriate name for this typical guest house: a relaxed, casual, friendly, informal hostelry that has been welcoming the same guests back for over twenty years. This guest house, however, happens to convey a little more—a piece of local history. It was the late-1800s Governor's Mansion where Queen Wilhelmina and Princess Juliana stayed during WW II and was later used to house various other government VIP's. Today, the Pasanggrahan has the notable title of the oldest guest house or hotel on the island.

Located between the narrow, bustling main street of town that hosts the popular shops of St. Maarten and the white sand beach with picturesque sailboat views, the Dutch colonial guest house holds court under tall trees and boasts a long white veranda. The guest lounge is decorated in a few period antiques, and a portrait of Queen Wilhelmina dominates the room.

The Garden Cafe restaurant of the inn, pleasantly taken over by overgrown tropical gardens and coconut palms, is where all three meals are served. This outside dining area along the beach offers spectacular sunset views and is romantically lit by torches each night. It's a favorite "happy hour" spot for the local businesspeople and is becoming in demand for wedding receptions because of its romantic views.

The guestrooms at the guest house are located alongside the Cafe in a two-story building, in a brand new annex building, and upstairs in the mansion itself. The informal tropical shrubbery surrounds and adds privacy to the guest quarters that all boast private, tiled shower baths

Pasanggrahan Royal Guest House, St. Maarten

and ceiling fans. A few of the rooms have air conditioning, kitchenettes, four-poster or king size beds, and all have attractive Guatemalan batik bedspreads with matching wall panels. The simple, pleasant decor includes a few antiques.

✺

Also on the Island

Oyster Pond Yacht Club
P.O. Box 239, Philipsburg, St. Maarten,
Netherlands Antilles

Phone: (011–599) 52–2206
Representative: David B. Mitchell & Co.

This castle-looking inn with towers and curved stone walls sits high on a promontory on the remote eastern edge of the island. It's a very exclusive hideaway, with prices on-season in the deluxe range. There are twenty original rooms surrounding a central courtyard, and twenty new rooms—called Oceanview Suites—set out on the bluff. The latter are well-equipped with cable televisions, refrigerators, telephones, ceiling fans, and air conditioning. Each one has a balcony. The older rooms are attractively decorated with white wicker from France, including rockers and peacock headboards. Guests can enjoy all three

Oyster Pond Yacht Club, St. Maarten

meals from a gourmet French menu, a mile-long beach, a pool carved out of coral, and the hotel's two tennis courts.

✳

St. Eustatius

Referred to as the "Golden Rock," St. Eustatius or "Statia" was once the trading hub of the Caribbean. The eight-mile-square dot thirty minutes by air from St. Maarten has two extinct volcanoes, the Quill and Little Mountain, with sweet potato and yam fields nestled in between. The climate is drier than Saba's, but the island enjoys fresh prevailing sea winds. Statia's prosperity waned when it was no longer needed as a transit port for American colonies; today, the Golden Rock is trying to shine again with a growing tourism trade.

Sightseeing, hiking, and beach-going are the most popular pastimes on the tiny, informal island. Car rentals or taxis will take the visitor around the island; vehicles travel American-style to the right. A visit to the cliff-perched capital city of Oranjestad will reveal eighteenth-century buildings and Fort Oranje, the present seat of island government and the former defender of security. Some of the original seventeenth- and eighteenth-century buildings that were situated on the waterfront have sunk into the sea and have become a major attraction for scuba divers and snorkelers.

The Quill, a volcano with an exceptionally beautiful rain forest in its crater, can be reached by burro with a guide. For a unique activity, visitors may hunt giant crabs here by moonlight and bring them back to town for tempting stuffed crab dishes. Another point of ecological distinction for Statia is the twice-a-year beaching of sea turtles here while they lay their eggs.

✳

The Old Gin House
P.O. Box 172, St. Eustatius, Netherlands Antilles

Phone: (011–599) 38–2319
Representative: E & M Associates
Key: Historic inn; 20 units; Expensive/Moderate EP; AE, VI, DC, MC.
Location: On beach; Near town; 1 mi. to airport.

A charming pair of inns has been reconstructed with historical authenticity and personal comfort guiding the way on the site of a 1700s warehouse and cotton gin, now filled with bougainvillea and palm trees. Ex-New York advertising executive John May and his late partner, Marty Scofield, are responsible for the stunning results in their quest to provide a truly pressure-free getaway for other executives amid history, charm, gourmet food, and modern conveniences—a blending almost too ideal, but one they aptly succeeded in achieving. The establishments, which are located across the road from each other, enable guests to mingle back and forth between the properties, partaking of their individual offerings.

The Old Gin House was the original transformation and the pair's inspiration. The nineteenth-century cotton gin factory was actually a conversion from a 1710-built warehouse. Located right on the beach at Oranjestad, the site was an ideal spot for their lodging endeavor. Brick ballast brought from Holland was used in the construction of the inn. Guestrooms boast balconies facing the sea.

The Old Gin House proved so popular that the owners purchased what was to become the Mooshay Bay Publick House just across the road. This old stone-constructed building is reminiscent of an eighteenth-century structure and is located on the ruins of an original molasses warehouse. The age-worn cistern on the property was transformed into an inviting little swimming pool, and the overseer's gallery is a charming library and backgammon room, abrim with warm antiques and island memorabilia.

The twenty guest accommodations can all be rated excellent in comfort, decor, and modern conveniences. Antiques, mainly from the eighteenth century, are tastefully mixed with practical pieces and locally handcrafted items at the Old Gin House; the modern, private bathrooms at both inns boast hot water showers. Guestrooms at Mooshay are furnished mainly with handmade island furniture and offer rooms that overlook the swimming pool and lush, tropical gardens. Paintings, flowering pots on terraces, and gentle colors all contribute to the sophisticated feel of each room's setting.

The Mooshay Publick House's dining room is the splendid locale of the inn's gourmet dinners. Classical music and candlelight set the tone for each evening's selected menu, served on delicate Delft china. (The inn's cuisine was featured as a cover story in *Gourmet* back in 1979.) Dinner is served among the rafters and bare brick walls. Breakfast and lunch are served on the beachfront terrace decorated in maritime antiques and surrounded by palms and ferns.

The pace at the Old Gin House and Mooshay Bay is casual and

relaxing, the service sublime, and the setting beautifully nostalgic.

Note: The inns are closed September 1 through October 15. At press time, the properties were expected to be sold.

French West Indies

LA DESIRADE

Point-a-Pitre

Gosier   St. Anne

GUADELOUPE

Basse Terre

Grand Case   ST. MARTIN

ST. BARTHELEMY
Gustavia

LES SAINTES   MARIE GALANTE

Basse-Pointe

Sainte Marie

Trinite

MARTINIQUE

Fort-de-France

St. Anne

N

Martinique, Guadeloupe, St. Martin (French-side), St. Barthelemy, and a small scattering of tiny offshore islands make up the French West Indies, a part of France itself and not merely colonies of the European nation. The ambience of France lends itself beautifully to these tropical isles located in the curve of the Lesser Antilles.

Regularly scheduled flights from North America arrive here daily; U.S. citizens are required to show a valid passport and a return ticket for entry. On the islands, taxis operate on set rates per car for up to four persons, with rates slightly higher at night. It is wise to settle upon the exact fare before leaving for your destination. The roads in the French West Indies are fairly good and car rental agencies are plentiful. Driving is American-style with traffic on the right, and the primary rule of the road is that priority always goes to the vehicle on the right. Gasoline prices are higher here, but the cars are economy models. Also note that no speed limits are set, and the French drivers tend to be impatient. Organized tours by cars or buses go to all parts of the islands, and various sailing vessels and boats offer trips to the French Indies' offshore islands.

The beautiful, tropical climate of the French West Indies is cooled year-round by *les alizes* or trade winds. Slightly wetter weather can occur September through November, but it lasts only briefly with lots of sunshine.

French, the national language of the islands, is tempered with an interesting Creole dialect. The French tourist bureau suggests that the visitor take along a phrase book, and they furnish one as well, which is a good idea since a majority of the population does not speak English. The currency is the French franc, but American dollars, traveler's checks, and credit cards are accepted widely. The electricity is 220 volts and requires a converter, available at some inns, to operate North American appliances.

Beach nudity or the European fashion of "topless" is often associated with the French West Indies islands. The visitor should be aware that there are no beaches reserved for nudists on Martinique and the practice is not permitted on public beaches. The topless fashion is prevalent at many hotels and on some of the beaches. There are a few designated nudist beaches on the island of Guadeloupe.

For additional information on the French West Indies contact:

French West Indies Tourist Board
610 Fifth Avenue, 5th floor
New York, NY 10020
(212) 757–1125

or

French Government Tourist Office
9401 Wilshire Blvd., Suite 303
Beverly Hills, CA 90212
(213) 271–6665

✻

Martinique

The Carib Indians originally named Martinique *Madinina,* meaning "island of flowers," and it lives up to its name with a rich, plentiful offering of tropical flowers and plants. Colorful hibiscus, rose laurels, oleander, bougainvillea, and more are accompanied by hummingbirds, turtledoves, tiny frogs, "forest kids," and crickets that provide magical background music to the tropical evening lit up by fireflies. The island is also submerged in a profusion of palm, bamboo, mahogany, mango, orange, pineapple, and papaya trees, as well as endless fields of sugar cane.

Martinique, population 345,000, has been a French Department since 1946, and its rich history is displayed in the numerous monuments and remains scattered about the island. Its 417 square miles of land are surrounded by white beaches, with five bays and dozens of coves, and rise gradually to mountains connected by hills called *mornes.*

Fort de France, the island's capital, is a bustling city bathed in pastel shades. Historic Fort Saint Louis stands guard over the boat-filled harbor where nearby open-markets are held. In the center of town is La Savane, a flower- and fountain-filled park with a white marble statue of the Empress Josephine. Overlooking the city are two more forts from the eighteenth and nineteenth centuries, as well as Sacre-Coeur de Balata, a miniature version of the basilica in Montmartre. The beautiful high-cheekboned, statuesque women of Martinique, clothed in sophisticated fashions or in the island's colorful red, green, and orange plaid, can be seen on the city's busy shopping streets.

Martinique offers many interesting and picturesque towns to explore and well-signed roads to make the sightseeing enjoyable.

The towns of Sainte-Anne and Sainte-Luce boast magnificent white sand beaches and nearby forests. Rivere Pilote, on the way to Sainte-Anne, is a charming village with European flavor and turn-of-the-century lightposts. The "Little Paris of the West Indies," Saint-Pierre, was the capital of Martinique until 1902 when Mt. Pelee erupted, killing all but one of its inhabitants. Ruins and relics of the town can be viewed on the spot and at the Franck A. Perret museum. Also, the birthplace of Empress Josephine and a sugar mill and church from 1765 may be found in the town of Trois-Ilets.

The island is known for its fine cuisine, both creole and French or a combination of the two. Dining often begins with a *petit punch blanc/vieux*, meaning punch made of light or dark rum with sugar cane syrup, lime (only for the tourists), and ice. Besides fine restaurants, Martinique offers an array of nightlife, with two casinos and several cabarets and discotheques.

Outdoor activities are plentiful on Martinique. Ample coral beds and reefs make underwater exploration popular. Fort de France is known as one of the safest and most beautiful bays in the Caribbean for sailing and yachting. Martinique offers a championship 140-acre golf course at La Pointe du Bout. The golfer can take a break here with a Planter's Punch while rocking leisurely in one of the clubhouse rocking chairs.

Relatively recent is the island's Regional Natural Park, covering 232 square miles, or half the island's total area. This park area has been developed to provide hiking, camping, horseback riding, and nature excursions for both the residents and the island's visitors.

Martinique time is one hour later than Eastern Standard Time. However, when the East Coast is on Eastern Daylight Time, Martinique and East Coast time is the same.

✳

Manoir de Beauregard
97227 Sainte-Anne, Martinique,
French West Indies

Phone: (011–596) 76–73–40
Representative: Robert Reid Associates
Key: Historic inn; 32 units; Inexpensive/Inexpensive CP; AE, MC, DC.
Location: Near town; 2 mi. to beach; 26 mi. to airport.

On a sunny hill just above the quaint seaside town of Sainte-Anne is this impressive eighteenth-century manor house-turned-inn-and-restaurant. A picturesque drive through small towns and pretty countryside brings you to this tranquil resort near one of the finest beaches in Martinique. The manor was built in the early 1700s and

Manoir de Beauregard, Martinique

may have been named after one of the first owner's daughters who married a knight named de la Touche de Beauregard. Although the history of the estate is still being researched, the idea of preserving the house and its contents was a high priority when the inn conversion took place a few years ago.

The manor house sits on a quiet piece of the countryside with panoramic views of the hills and trees. The tropical growth is informal and dotted with small sitting areas that take advantage of the quiet. The manor house, containing all but five of the guest accommodations, is white with old stone and wooden shutter detailing. You enter the house through a side door that is fronted by a colorful parrot in a cage. The first impression of the almost cavernous reception room and lounge is that of an old castle or perhaps a church. The marble-tiled floor is the original and the stone walls are untouched, only accented with old portraits and rich tapestries. Deep, arched recesses are filled with antique settees, cane rocking chairs, and a grandfather's clock, and a scrolled, green iron grating with gold leaf that once graced a nineteenth-century church now forms doors and staircase railings. The polished wood-beamed ceilings of the two common areas hold spectacular gilded chandeliers.

The restaurant of the inn connects to the far side of the lounge, mingling the old and the new. The spacious room with pleasant cross breezes is decorated in a few antique hoosiers displaying china and in several tables with straw chair seating. The tables are gaily covered in a

Martinique-plaid. All three meals are served in the restaurant; the complimentary breakfast for guests includes a continental fare of juice, fresh fruit, rolls, and coffee. To the left of the lounge is a small boutique selling handsome hand-painted items of silk.

All of the guestrooms at Manoir de Beauregard boast private baths, air conditioning, and telephones, and all of the guest accommodations in the manor house happily boast antique decor. In fact, most of the furniture in the house is authentic and entirely handmade of native wood; these pieces are at least 100 years old. One room downstairs holds identical double four-poster beds, an antique rocker, and dressers. French doors lead to the room's own private patio overlooking the pool and hills. Upstairs rooms are reached through halls spiced with antique pieces, prints, and attractive flower arrangements from the gardens.

Though lacking the charm of the manor house, a few additional guestrooms are available in a row building to the rear of the house. This building, covered in pink and yellow tropical blooms, has five guestrooms with more standard, contemporary decor.

Horseback riding is available at the estate, and an inviting L-shaped pool to the front of the old house offers the same pastoral views. Just a few minutes drive away is a beautiful white sand beach that might cause you to divide your time between this serene resort and its warm blue water.

✳

Plantation de Leyritz
97218 Basse-Pointe, Martinique, French West Indies

Phone: (011–596) 78–53–92; (800) 366–9815 or (800) 366–1510
Representative: Jacques de Larsay and International Travel & Resorts
Key: Plantation; 71 units; Moderate/Moderate CP; VI, MC, AE.
Location: Countryside; 15 mi. to beach; 35 mi. to airport.

A scenic drive through winding roads lined with lush tropical vegetation and small towns leads to a smaller road that bumps past banana fields to this charming sixteen-acre plantation resort. On a secluded hill overlooking the Atlantic in the distance, Plantation de Leyritz feels remote and displaced from the rest of the world, wrapped in eighteenth-century history and working agricultural fields. Of course, this

Plantation de Leyritz, Martinique

ideal picture is not at all times serene since the plantation is a favorite of bus tour passengers, who travel miles to sample the delicious French cuisine and soak up the centuries of history and sheer beauty of the location. Fortunately there is enough tranquility and beauty to share with the occasional day-visitor here.

The plantation was built around 1700 and has been restored lovingly by the present owners. At the core of the plantation is the original planter's house with twenty-inch-thick stone walls, beamed ceilings, tile and flagstone floors, and an expensive and rare Vienna wood staircase. The coral-colored building with old wooden shutters and shingled roof holds a gracious parlor with beautifully restored antiques and Oriental rugs. In fact, the antique parlor dining table, flanked by antique china cabinets with silver pieces and rich, old paintings, was the site of the 1974 Meeting of the Presidents with presidents Ford and Giscard d'Estaing in attendance. Located upstairs are ten antique-filled guestrooms that evoke the true flavor of this eighteenth century plantation resort.

The rest of the guest accommodations at the plantation are located in various impeccably restored cottages that surround the grounds, most of those former slave quarters. One especially attractive unit was the former kitchen of the plantation and grants spectacular views. The various wood shingle- and stone-constructed buildings are decorated in a mixture of antiques and contemporary decor, but mostly convey an antique feel. All of the guest accommodations are different, but commonly offer private bathrooms, air conditioning, and telephones.

A formal French garden offers some of the best views over the banana fields and the pretty plantation swimming pool with antique marble dolphins. Two fountains, one a waterfall and the other a basin, highlight the botanical gardens that boast trees with name plaques, bright red poinsettias, and traveler's palms.

Fronted by a flowing, manicured lawn and fish ponds is the plantation's restaurant, a former rum and sugar factory. The elegant stone dining rooms contain rough wooden beams overhead, remnants of an old chapel, and red anthuriums clinging to the ancient walls. An ever-flowing sheet of water gurgles down one of the old walls, a natural waterfall when it rains and a motor-driven flow on sunny days. The effect is soothing, and the food is a sublime offering of French and creole delectables. Guests at Leyritz are treated to a complimentary breakfast here, and lunch and dinner are also available. The gourmet dishes include such entrees as coconut milk chicken, pork flambee, and various "colombos" or stews.

The Plantation de Leyritz has recently opened a health spa on the premises. Special spa programs that include diet and beauty treatments are available, and a doctor is in residence at this unique health farm. Twenty-one new spa rooms decorated in antiques are in the new two-story spa building located across a covered path.

✳

Rivage Hotel
P.O. Box 45, Anse Mitan Trois Ilets, 97229 Martinique, French West Indies

Phone: (011–596) 66–00–53
Key: Inn; 17 units; Moderate/Inexpensive CP; Credit cards accepted.
Location: Near beach; Near town; 20 min. to airport.

Located across the road from a beach, the Rivage is a small, intimately-run inn. Maryelle and Jean-Claude Riveti are the hospitable owners and take pride in offering bargain rates along with a complimentary breakfast, welcome drink, and lots of personal service. Maryelle makes international travelers feel comfortable with her knowledge of French, English, Spanish, and Creole on this primarily French-speaking island.

The hotel has a pretty lawn area with lots of tropical foliage, a free-form swimming pool surrounded by rocking chairs and tables and chairs for outside eating or drinking, and a barbecue for guests. The reception area offers a television set and a nice selection of games for guests' use, and Hertz car rentals may be handled here as well. Breakfast, lunch, and dinner are served in the snack bar, and a daily special is among the offerings. Your welcome drink is served in the inn's own "Latanier Bar."

Other sports nearby include fishing (with the inn supplying the fishing poles), boat rentals, tennis, golf, and horseback riding. For your convenience various excursions may be arranged at the reception desk by your friendly hosts.

✳

Saint Aubin Hotel
P.O. Box 52, 97220 Trinite, Martinique,
French West Indies

Phone: (011–596) 69–34–77
Key: Historic inn; 15 units; Inexpensive/Inexpensive EP; AE, DC, VI, MC.
Location: 1 mi. to beach; 3 mi. to town; 20 mi. to airport.

This recently restored gingerbread-laden, pink Victorian is perched majestically on a hill overlooking the Atlantic. A drive curves gently up to the house and is lined with colorful flowers and turn-of-the-century lamp globes mounted on palm tree bases. The front of the house bears a gracious circular driveway with pink flowers in the center planter and green wrought-iron gates that protect the privacy of the estate. An outside veranda with gleaming tile, scalloped pillars, and green wrought-iron trim decorates the house itself.

The 1900-built home was rebuilt on the old plantation site that dates back to the seventeenth century. The comfortable inn with quality food is the result of several years of Mr. Foret Guy's hard work. He is the bed and breakfast's hospitable owner and manager, and he gives each letter and special request his personal attention.

The bottom floor of the house has a small reception area and guest parlor, as well as the inn's dining room off a quaint pair of French doors. Old-fashioned globe chandeliers, a small bar, television, and some wicker furnishings fill the parlor and reception areas, while the dining area offers more traditional furnishings with seating for fifty on

Saint Aubin Hotel, Martinique

antique tables and chairs. The comfortable room boasts built-in hutch-es, pillared woodwork, and unusual two-tone, inlaid wooden floors. The dining room, with views of the ocean, is just for guests of the inn and features a complimentary continental breakfast and a complete and tasty creole and French dinner menu. Lunches are not available.

The fifteen guestrooms of the St. Aubin are located on the second and third levels of the house. A fancy white-spooled banister with oak trim leads upstairs. The second-level landing is the site of an unusual mini-flight of stairs that leads out to the veranda with panoramic views of the lush hills. All the rooms on this floor open onto the veranda.

The guestrooms at the inn have all been modernized with air conditioning, wall-to-wall carpeting, up-to-date and private bath-rooms, telephones, and attractive wallcoverings. The guest quarters do not possess the antique charm of the house in terms of furnishings, but are very clean and comfortable. Guestrooms on the third floor, the former attic of the home, contain units that can accommodate up to four people and boast homey slanted ceilings with wallpaper cover-ings.

The rear grounds of the St. Aubin are as quite and delightful as the front. An informal flower garden, wide grassy lawn, and swimming pool with cabana occupy the back acreage in this intimate and hos-pitable spot.

*

Also on the Island

Hotel Victoria
Rond Pointe de Didier, P.O. Box 337, Fort-de-France,
Martinique, French West Indies

Phone: (011–596) 60–56–78

Located in a residential area of the city, this medium-size inn offers thirty guest accommodations and views of the harbor. The main house is a nineteenth-century colonial structure, but all the guestrooms are contained in small bungalows on the grounds. Each bungalow is air conditioned and decorated simply yet comfortably. A gingerbread-adorned veranda on the house is a pleasant spot from which to watch the bay while enjoying a drink from the bar. A garden swimming pool is available for guests, as well as a comfortable parlor with television. A restaurant serving delicious French specialties is a part of this family-owned hotel that is gaining a large repeat business.

※

Guadeloupe

The Carib Indians who originally inhabited this island named it "island of beautiful waters," which is very true of butterfly-shaped Guadeloupe. This "double" island's parts are separated by a drawbridge and narrow strait called *La Riviere Salee.* Grand-Terre is characterized by rolling hills and ample sugar plantations, while Basse-Terre to the west is mountainous and banana plantation- and forest-filled with a dormant volcano, La Soufriere. Guadeloupe, 580 square miles in size, has several island dependencies: Iles des Saintes, Marie Galante, and La Desirade, all offshore, and the islands of St. Barthelemy and French St. Martin, which are discussed here independently.

Basse-Terre, the city, is the capital of the island, but the larger city of Point-a-Pitre on the southwest coast of Grande-Terre is the commercial center of activity. Point-a-Pitre, often called the "Paris of the Antilles," is a modern, crowded city lacking a French old-world charm; instead it is full of modern apartments and condominiums. This port city has some shopping significance, a nineteenth-century cathedral, and some scenic squares. The open-air markets and boutique stalls around the narrow streets contain colorful displays of the local wares. Three miles east of Point-a-Pitre is the Fort Fluer d'Epee, an eighteenth-century fortress offering spectacular views of the city and the nearby offshore islands.

Other spots to visit on Guadeloupe might include Sainte-Anne, a quaint village with a town hall, church, and nearby beaches; Pointes-des-Chateaux, a castlelike rock formation with coved beaches; Les Chutes du Carbet, a trio of waterfalls near the town of St. Sauveur; and La Soufriere, Guadeloupe's steam-breathing volcano. The foot of the volcano's crater can be reached by car and the rim is reached by foot trails, marked in colors for ease. The walking part of the trip can take up to three hours and a guide is recommended. St. Claude is an interesting town at the base of the volcano. The town, dotted with interesting colonial architecture, is worth the visit.

A few stretches of white sand make swimming and sunning a pastime in Guadeloupe, but the surf on some of the island's beaches is too wild for safe swimming. An area off Pigeon Island, frequented by Jacques Cousteau, is considered one of the top scuba and diving spots in the Caribbean. For those looking inland, the Parc Natureal provides excellent hiking trails through rain forests sprinkled with waterfalls and pools.

The nightlife of Guadeloupe is accented by its dancing; Guadeloupeans claim to have begun the beguine. A casino and several clubs come alive at night. Guadeloupe offers creole cuisine and not the classic French dishes of neighboring Martinique. The island celebrates its culinary art each year at the Cook's Festival, characterized by a parade, music, and dancing, as well as a huge feast enduring several hours.

A tour or independent plane-hop trip to Guadeloupe's offshore islands of Iles des Saintes and Marie Galante provides wonderful sightseeing and delicate fine white beaches. Sugar mills, rolling hills, and architecturally quaint towns and squares make for wonderful strolling and picnicking.

Guadeloupe time is one hour later than Eastern Standard Time and the same as Eastern Daylight Time.

✳

Hamak
97118 Saint-Francois, Guadeloupe,
French West Indies

Phone: (011–590) 88–59–99
Representative: David B. Mitchell & Company; Jacques de Larsay
Key: Inn; 56 units; Deluxe/Deluxe CP; AE, MC, VI, DC.
Location: On beach; 20 miles from airport.

Back in 1979, Jimmy Carter and friends held their four-nation Summit Meeting at Hamak, a small, exclusive hotel tucked away on Guadeloupe's southeastern coast. It's easy to see why. This marvelous remote hotel offers lots of privacy; guests stay in individual bungalows that are smothered in bougainvillea and hibiscus blossoms. Each one has its own patio—with a hammock, of course. The whole complex is smack-dab on a sun-bleached beach planted with long-trunked palms, fronted by a sea as green as pistachio ice cream.

Visitors wishing to do more than swing in hammocks, sip frosty drinks, and brown themselves on the beach can take their pick of active diversions. A Robert Trent Jones golf course is across the road, as are tennis and water sports.

✳

Relais du Moulin
Chateaubrun, Sainte-Anne 97180, Guadeloupe,
French West Indies

Phone: (011–590) 88–23–96
Key: Plantation; 40 units; Moderate/Inexpensive CP; AE, VI, MC.
Location: Countryside; 1 mi. to beach; 18 mi. to airport.

After a pleasant drive out of the town of Sainte-Anne, traveling through a picturesque countryside, you will spot a windmill ruin in the midst of green fields. Look carefully for a sign that will lead you through a palm-lined drive to the sugar mill ruin, now reception office, of the Relais du Moulin. This circular stone building was built in 1843 as a part of the working sugar plantation. The mill boasts pretty stone

Relais du Moulin, Guadeloupe

arches and a low wall at its base, which overflows with purple bougainvillea. A steel spiral staircase makes the climb to the top of the old mill easy and most worthwhile. The 360-degree views from this historic ruin take in the lush countryside and ocean for as far as you can see. The only sounds you hear in this tranquil setting, except for your fellow guests, are the mill's blades cutting through the ocean breezes as they spin around most of the day.

Although the encompassing views from atop the windmill are not available from the remainder of the inn's facilities, the green, tranquil countryside most certainly is. An outdoor bar surrounded by tropical vegetation sits next to the mill and serves drinks in its setting of pretty tilework and beamed ceilings; the inn's cat pays an occasional friendly visit. Across from the bar is the inn's Tap-Tap Restaurant. This enclosed and spacious eating area has the same elaborate beamed ceiling and handsome decor marked by green high-back chairs and pastel tropical-print tablecloths. The walls carry paintings and old photographs of the sugar mill, and the table centerpieces are miniature "tap-taps," or colorful buses. The complimentary morning breakfast of rolls, juice, and fruit is served to guests here, along with lunch and dinner.

A few steps down from the bar and restaurant area is the swimming pool, hidden by fragrant tropical foliage. Surrounded by lounges, the blue-tiled pool is most inviting and a popular gathering spot. This country inn also offers archery and horseback riding to its guests; a long beach is about a ten-minute walk away through fields, but the surf tends to be a bit wild.

The guestrooms at the Relais du Moulin are all contained in bungalows to the rear of the mill and restaurant/bar area. Each unit is quite private and named after a different flower. The units, which are all similar, are actually mini-suites, with a small living room with two daybeds and refrigerator, separate bedroom with double bed or twins, private bath with modern facilities, and shower and private patio. These suites are pint-sized and decorated sparsely in a contemporary mode. The floors are of linoleum, the walls are pine paneled, the ceiling is a dropped acoustic type, and the drapery is grass cloth. The bathrooms carry a bit more charm, with pretty wallcoverings and hand-painted tile. Probably the most alluring feature of the room units are the patios that sit right in the flower-filled fields. The views are tranquil, but the field-enclosed setting does invite a bit of the outdoors in. It is quite advisable to take along your insect repellent when visiting this country oasis.

✻

Also on the Island

Auberge de la Vielle Tour
97190 Gosier, Guadeloupe, French West Indies

Phone: (011–590) 84–23–23
Representative: Pullman International Hotels

This eighty-room hotel is magnificently situated on a hill overlooking the water. Its rooms are all tucked away in the hillside, surrounded by greens and fragrant blossoms. All are well-equipped with minibars, televisions, air conditioners, and balconies overlooking the gardens and beach area.

There are three beaches to take your pick of, though the hotel does arrange boat trips to nearby islands for those who really want to get away (complete with picnics prepared by the hotel chef). In addition, there are a pool and three tennis courts, which are lit at night.

The real attraction here, however, is the restaurant, considered one of the finest on the island. Though the French nouvelle menu changes periodically, it always offers lots of seafood and fish dishes with very innovative sauces and accompaniments.

✻

Les Saintes

It's hard to believe that there are places in the Caribbean that haven't been discovered, but this tiny archipelago fits the bill. On Terre-de-Haut, the only island with any hotels, the big event of the day is the arrival of the boat from Guadeloupe bringing tourists and produce. All the locals flock to the dock to watch. Barefoot children with cotton dresses dangle baskets of *Tourments d'Amour* (agony of love)—sweet little coconut tarts. Toothless fishermen stand holding their nets. Space becomes a commodity on the steps of the church everyone has to pass to get to the heart of town. Tourists scatter about on mopeds (shakily at first) or in one of the island's few tourist buses. You won't see many cars here; everyone walks, bicycles, or putts around on mopeds. Bourg is a lovable town, made up of smartly painted little wood houses. There are a handful of shops to explore, as well as a waterfront market crammed with all sorts of unrecognizable fruits and vegetables.

There are several beaches tucked away in inlets all around the island. One of the most popular is Pont-Pierre, where everyone from bare-bottomed babies to blond—yes, *blond*—Rastafarians—seems to have a good time. At sunset one night, make your way up to Le Chameau, the high point of the island and, inevitably, the high point of your trip. A stone citadel crowns a hilltop, giving you a 360-degree view. Keeping up with the French West Indies' high culinary standards, Terre-de-Haut boasts some exceptionally good restaurants.

✳

Auberge des Anacardiers
La Savane, 97137 Terre-de-Haut, Les Saintes,
French West Indies

Phone: (011–590) 99–50–99
Representative: Jacques de Larsay
Key: Inn; 10 units; Moderate/Moderate MAP; AE, MC, VI.
Location: On a hilltop, five minutes by hotel mini-bus from town and dock.

One of Terre-de-Haut's brochures refers to it as "Le Dernier Paradis." Indeed, this small inn feels like the last paradise.

It's beautifully set on a hilltop surrounded by sweet-smelling flowers. All ten rooms are very French and very lovely, full of mahogany furnishings.

The only drawback is that it's not smack dab on the beach. But on such a small island, this is never a problem. Besides, there is a pool set into the hillside, just waiting to be rippled.

Dining in the front parlor is *extraordinaire* with, of course, lots of seafood and fish prepared with French flair. The little touches at Auberge des Anacardiers—a cage of doves, French music—make this a very special *auberge*.

✳

Also on the Island
Le Village Creole
Point Coquelet, Terre-de-Haut, 97137 Les Saintes, French West Indies

Phone: (011–590) 99–53–83

Located right on the water, Le Village Creole has a series of eleven cottages that house twenty-two duplex suites. Each one is simply furnished and equipped with a full kitchen, separate bedrooms and living room, and a garden patio.

✳

St. Barthelemy

This tiny, 8½-mile-square island, commonly referred to as St. Barts, is full of natural, uncrowded beauty, and it is distinguished by a Swedish influence. The beautiful green mountains and coral sand beaches combine with its toy-scaled capital, Gustavia, to make it a special spot in the Caribbean.

Discovered by Columbus in 1493, the islands was named after his brother Bartholomew and settled by the French in 1648. In 1784 Louis XVI traded St. Barts to Sweden for a warehouse. The Swedes rechristened its capital Gustavia and made the island a rich trade port until 1878, when France took control of it once again.

Gustavia, home to 90 percent of the 3,500 population, includes descendants of Norman, Breton, and Poitevin settlers. The harbor town is quaint and neat with Swedish Colonial and French Creole structures and French boutiques that attract the visitors. There are several small cafes for snacks and refreshments.

The town of Corossol, referred to as the "straw village," on the northwest end of the island is famous for its descendants of early French days who dress in white bonnets and sell fine straw hats and other straw souvenirs that are woven from the leaf fibers of the fan palms.

St. Barts also offers a touch of St. Tropez in its beach and cafe-life. The nights are slow and dedicated to dining and wine and just relaxing. The Festival of St. Barthelemy is a French country fair with a definite tropical influence that is held each August. Gustavia is then filled with booths, sports, and lots of parties.

You can reach St. Barts by taking a small aircraft from nearby islands, on a one-hour flight from Guadeloupe, or by taking a catamaran from Philipsburg. St. Barts is on Atlantic Standard Time all year and has the same time as the East Coast during Eastern Daylight Saving season.

✳

Sapore Di Mare
Box 60, Mt. Lurin 97133, St. Barthelemy,
French West Indies

Phone: (011–590) 27–61–73; (212) 319–7488
Representative: Jane Martin
Key: Inn; 10 units; Expensive-Deluxe/Expensive-Deluxe CP; AE, MC, VI in restaurant only.
Location: In the hills, ³/₄ mi. from Gustavia; 1.7 mi. from airport.

Set apart in a world of its own, Sapore Di Mare (the former Castelets) surveys the island from its mountain peak location. It's important to reserve well in advance, as its ten units (including duplex villas and rooms) fill quickly. All are exquisitely decorated with antiques and have broad terraces with bewitching 180-degree views. The villas have two bedrooms, complete kitchens, and tape decks. For years, this hilltop hotel has been a retreat for film makers, actors, ballet stars (including Mikhail Baryshnikov), writers, and other visitors who consider it a home-away-from-home.

With new owners, the hotel remains largely unchanged except for the restaurant which is now a culinary playground for Pino Luongo, an Italian chef who introduced innovative Tuscan cuisine to the U.S. in two very successful New York restaurants. Since there are no Italian West Indies, this is a welcome addition to the islands. Favorite dishes include *cacciucco alla toscana*, a spicy seafood stew, and *fettuccine al sugo di aragosta*, homemade fettuccine tossed with lobster, tomato, cream, and crushed red pepper.

While staying at Sapore Di Mare, it's a good idea to rent a Mini-Moke (a Jeep-like vehicle) to get to the beach (about a seven-minute ride away) and the island's other restaurants. You will, however, find a small pool at Sapore Di Mare.

✻

Hotel Manapany
Box 114, 97133 St. Barthelemy, French West Indies

Phone: (011–590) 27–75–28; (800) 847–4249; (212) 719–5750.
Representative: Mondotels
Key: Inn; 52 units; Deluxe/Expensive EP; AE, MC, VI.
Location: On water, 5 minute drive from airport.

Set right on the shores of Anse de Caye, the Hotel Manapany is a huddle of white-walled, red-roofed, gingerbread-trimmed cottages that gaze out to sea. Some are inches from the water's edge; others are carved out of the hillside that crowds around it. Each one has both a suite and a double room tropically decorated with fresh whites and pastels and wicker furniture. The suites have screened-in porches and kitchenettes; the rooms have balconies.

Dining is exceptional in both of the hotel's restaurants, one concentrating on French, the other on Italian cuisine. The French restaurant—Ballahou—is considered one of St. Bart's best (on an island of French restaurants, that's quite a compliment). Still, you might especially enjoy the latter—the glass-enclosed Ouanalou—since there are no Italian West Indies. For working it all off, there's a tennis court (with lights) and an exercise room with Universal equipment, but most guests divide their time between the pool and the beach.

✻

Hotel Guanahani
Anse de Grand Cul-de-Sac, 97133 St. Barthelemy, French West Indies

Phone: (011–590) 27–66–60
Representative: Leading Hotels of the World; Crown International WIMCO
Key: Inn; 68 rooms; Deluxe/Deluxe EP; AE, MC, VI.
Location: On Grand Cul-de-Sac Bay; 15 minutes from airport.

Though hardly big, the Hotel Guanahani is the largest hotel on St. Barts. It's also one of its newest, having opened in 1987.

Guanahani is perched on a peninsula overlooking a shallow bay that's always busy with windsurfers darting about. Its rooms and suites are all in pastel-colored gingerbread-trimmed West Indian-style cottages. Individual rooms range from deluxe doubles to two-bedroom suites; all with fans and air conditioning, refrigerators, satellite televisions, radios, telephones, and private balconies or patios with views of the sea. Some have kitchenettes and/or Jacuzzis.

There are two restaurants at Guanahani—the formal Bartolomeo and the poolside, French-style casual Indigo—both with sea views. Along with a beautiful beach, there's one main pool with a Jacuzzi and eleven smaller private or semiprivate pools scattered around the suites. There are also two tennis courts, lit for night play and a wide selection of water sports (windsurfing, HobieCats, fishing, sailing).

✳

El Sereno Beach Hotel
BP 19, 97133, St. Barthelemy, French West Indies

Phone: (011–590) 27–64–80
Representative: International Travel & Resorts, Inc.; Jacques de Larsay

This twenty-room hotel is beautifully set on a secluded beach and bay. It's a very tranquil spot, devoted to the leisure life. All the rooms are located in bungalows and have satellite television (VCR upon request), air conditioning, refrigerator, telephone, and private garden patio. Seventeen of them have garden views; three overlook the sea.

The restaurant—an open pavilion set alongside the beach—as well as the hotel itself, is overseen by Lyons-born owner/manager Marc Llepez and his spouse, Christine.

✳

Francois Plantation
Colombier, 97133, St. Barthelemy, French West Indies

Phone: (011–590) 27–78–89
Representative: WIMCO; Jacques de Larsay

Though not on the beach, this inland hotel—a collection of twelve cottages surrounded by beautiful greens and gardens—more than makes up for it with other appeals. All of the cottages are designed in traditional Antillean style and handsomely decorated with mahogany four-poster beds. Each has air conditioning, ceiling fan, cable television, wall safe, and mini-bar. The dining room, which is part of the old plantation that stood here, is the site of many a memorable meal, and, in fact, it is considered one of the island's best restaurants. There's a pool on the grounds, and the beach is within walking distance (well—second thought, you're better off with a car).

✳

St. Martin

The divided island of Saint Martin (Sint Maarteen in Dutch) is partly French and partly Dutch, with complete freedom of movement from area to area. Having coexisted peacefully for over 330 years, the two parts of the thirty-seven-square-mile island offer two cultures in one stop. The northern part of the island belongs to France and has about twenty-one square miles of area. French St. Martin, population 7,000, is governed from Guadeloupe; the principal town of Marigot is the seat of the municipal council.

Marigot is a tiny French village with a nearby fort offering views of the western part of the island. Most visitors here come for the shopping in the quaint boutiques, displaying all sorts of French finery and perfume. Grand Case, about thirty minutes away, is really a small fishing village with some good local restaurants specializing in creole cooking.

Although not as popular with tourists as the island's Dutch side, St. Martin is becoming a popular tourist destination with an emphasis on relaxation and friendliness. There are many fine beaches, some with nude bathing. The north end of the island has some good diving spots, and boats can be rented for deep-sea fishing.

St. Martin is on Atlantic Standard Time. During Eastern Daylight Time, the island and the East Coast are on the same time schedule.

*

Hotel Hevea
Grand Case, 97150, St. Martin, French West Indies

Phone: (011–590) 87–56–85
Representative: WIMCO
Key: Guest House; 8 units; Expensive/Inexpensive EP; MC, VI.
Location: In Grand Case, across the road from the beach, ten minutes drive from Marigot.

Located right in the one-street town of Grand Case, this is a wonderfully welcoming guest house, owned by Jacqueline and Jean-Claude Dalbera, who come from Nice. All the units—which include rooms, studios, and one apartment that sleeps four—are decorated West Indian style, painted in pastel colors, and immaculately kept. There are beamed ceilings, washstands, and carved wood beds covered by mosquito nets. Six of the accommodations have kitchenettes, all have air conditioning and private bathrooms. The dining room at Hotel Hevea is one of the best restaurants in town.

*

Also on the Island

Grand Case Beach Club
Box 339, Grand Case 97150, St. Martin, French West Indies

Phone: (011–590) 87–51–87; (800) 223–1588; (212) 661–4540

Guests find dozens of restaurants and more than enough water sports right at their fingertips at the Grand Case Beach Club, a condo complex set on one of St. Martin's prettiest slabs of beach. The seventy-five units that include studios and one- and two-bedroom apartments are attractively decorated with rattan furniture and equipped with kitchens and private patios; most have sea views.

British Windward Islands

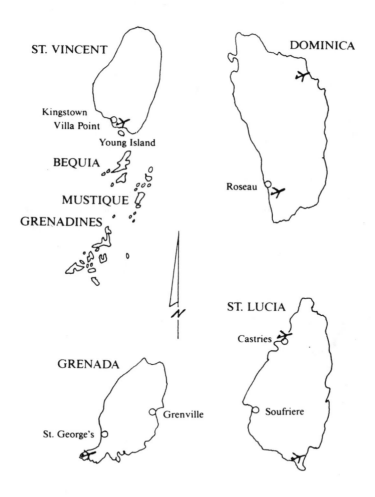

ST. VINCENT

DOMINICA

Kingstown
Villa Point
Young Island

BEQUIA

Roseau

MUSTIQUE

GRENADINES

ST. LUCIA

Castries

GRENADA

Grenville

Soufriere

St. George's

N

*T*hese small, lushly green and mountainous islands are cooled by the ever-present northeasterly trade winds. The British Windwards, consisting of the islands of Dominica, St. Lucia, St. Vincent, Grenada, and The Grenadines, are now predominantly British-affiliated, but retain influences of past Gallic or French inhabitants.

The Eastern Caribbean dollar or the "BeeWee" is the monetary currency on all of these islands, and the electrical voltage requires an adapter for North American appliances. The British Windward Islands are on Atlantic Standard Time but share the same time as the East Coast during Eastern Daylight Saving Time months.

✳

St. Vincent and The Grenadines

St. Vincent and the Grenadines is a collection of thirty-two main islands and cays and numerous smaller ones scattered in the Eastern Caribbean, 100 miles west of Barbados. St. Vincent, the largest, is eighteen miles long and eleven miles wide. To the southwest is the chain of smaller islands called The Grenadines, most of these islands no larger than a few square miles. Surrounded by white coral beaches and crystalline waters that range in color from sapphire blue to emerald green, the Grenadines are a diver's or snorkeler's paradise and provide superb sailing conditions.

Connecting flights to St. Vincent and The Grenadines are available from Barbados, St. Lucia, Martinique, or Trinidad, and several daily flights go inter-island to and from St. Vincent.

For further information on St. Vincent and The Grenadines contact:

Caribbean Tourist Organization
20 East 46th Street
New York, NY 10017
(212) 682–0435

✳

St. Vincent

This volcanic island is rich in fruit, vegetables, and spices. Its flatland interior, with coconuts, bananas, breadfruit, nutmeg, and arrowroot, contrasts with its steep mountain ridges, coastal cliffs, and rocky shores that dip down to the gold and black sand beaches.

Representing a real blending of cultures, descendants of the Carib Indians still live on the northern shores of La Soufriere. British and French cultures mix in their language and customs. English is the official language, and cricket and afternoon tea are traditions in St. Vincent.

Kingstown is the capital of the island and is a busy port and market town with twelve small blocks crammed with non-tourist, local shopping and commerce. Saturday morning market is colorful and well-stocked with fresh vegetables and fruit. St. Mary's Roman Cathedral, an example of old European architectures, and Fort Charlotte, offering magnificent views of The Grenadines, are both located in Kingstown. North of town are the Botanic Gardens, the oldest in the Western Hemisphere and occupying twenty acres filled with tropical trees, blossoms, and plants. Captain Bligh of the *Bounty* fame planted the breadfruit plants here in 1793. Also here is the Museum of Archeology, with an extensive collection of stone artifacts.

A boat trip to the northern tip of the island takes visitors to the Falls of Baleine, a sixty-foot freshwater fall with shallow pools at the base of the volcanic slopes. Hikers may climb 3¹/₂ miles up La Soufriere, St. Vincent's northern volcano, and be treated to spectacular views.

Sightseers can also visit several charming fishing villages to the west with their pastel-colored cottages and unusual black sand beaches. To tour St. Vincent a car can be rented with a small fee for a local license, but note that roads tend to be mountainous and curvy. Taxis are plentiful as well, but it is advisable to travel with a member of the island's Taxi Drivers' Association and decide upon a rate for the outing before departing.

✳

The Cobblestone Inn
P.O. Box 867, Kingstown, St. Vincent, West Indies

Phone: (809) 456–1937 or 456–1938
Key: Historic inn; 19 units; Expensive/Expensive CP; AE, VI.
Location: In town; 3 mi. to beach; 3 mi. to airport.

The Cobblestone Inn, a fine government-run bed and breakfast, dates back to 1814 when it was built as a sugar warehouse. Later it was

The Cobblestone Inn, St. Vincent

used to store arrowroot. The inn was converted to hotel use in 1972 when extensive renovation work exposed the Georgian architecture with its enchanting cobblestone walkways and arches. Local craftsmen utilized the same materials used in the original Georgian structure to complete the careful restoration.

The inn is situated directly on the waterfront in the small capital city of Kingstown and overlooks the harbor backed by the green mountainous scenery of the island. The bar and restaurant of the hotel are located on street level, right off the tiny but busy thoroughfare. The attractive eating and drinking areas boast the old stone walls and charming small-paned windows. The complimentary morning breakfast is served in the popular restaurant.

An airy stone stairway passage with green wrought-iron trim leads to the second-level reception desk and guestrooms. The guestrooms at the Cobblestone Inn are a nice blend of modern and old, with limestone-carved arches framing the windows and walls of old exposed stonework. The furnishings are all modern and attractive, featuring cane headboards, dressers, modern private baths, and telephones in the rooms. The accommodations are fully air conditioned and have become a favorite of business travelers because of the Cobblestone's pleasant furnishings and in-town convenience.

✳

Grand View Beach Hotel
Villa Point, P.O. Box 173, St. Vincent, West Indies

Phone: (809) 458–4811; (800) 223–5352
Representative: Robert Reid Associates
Key: Historic inn; 12 units; Deluxe/Deluxe CP; AE, VI, MC.
Location: On beach; 3¹/₂ mi. to town; 3 mi. to airport.

Located on Villa Point on the south coast of the island, this family-run inn offers spectacular ocean vistas, tranquility, and old-fashioned hospitality. The original 1860-built cotton drying house on eight acres of beautifully landscaped gardens became the estate home of owner Tony Sardine's wife's great grandparents. Tony's father bought the estate in 1930; Tony was born in the house. The Grand View became a charming family hotel in 1964 when Tony's father left his bakery in town to begin the lodging establishment. Tony took over the thriving business, now in its twenty-seventh year of operation—a delightful representation of a family operation spanning both sides of the Sardine family.

A scenic roadway climbs up to the point overlooking the bay and leads to the intimate resort. The inn's tennis and squash courts are to the side of the road on the way up to the house, as is a restful thatched gazebo lookout with views of the ocean and town. The villa house with brick

Grand View Beach Hotel, St. Vincent

175

arches and French windows is fronted by gardens highlighted by a tranquil fountain with lily ponds and by a large veranda-type open entry semi-attached to the house. The veranda, with polished tile floors and wood coverings, is a pleasant spot to sit and take in the views of the bay.

The entrance to the old home sets the tone of warmth found within. The neutral walls are trimmed in coral shades; a painting of the home as it originally looked is displayed in the hallway. The painting shows that a balcony once fronted the house, but reveals that the home's charm has not been lost through the years. The guest parlor of the house is decorated in pretty antiques and local wood furnishings made by the family. Books, magazines, and games are supplied; a corner nook displays antique china and silver pieces. Old family photos hang from the antique picture railing around the gracious room. Burgundy draperies and coordinated pillows give the room a warm turn-of-the-century feel. The beautiful wooden floors here and throughout the house are of local cedar; the polished wooden staircase banister to the second-story guestrooms is of rich mahogany.

The dozen upstairs guestrooms are each named after a flower found on the lush premises. The rooms all boast private baths and a sunny, airy feel. The decor is simple but cheery and comfortable. A pretty flower print of each room's namesake graces the walls, and rockers, vanities/desks, large closets, flowered curtains, straw-mat rugs, and telephones can be found in each room. The private, tiled bathrooms feature spacious shower stalls and very hot water. The guestrooms, in harmonious pastel shades of green, yellow, and white or blues and lilacs, offer spectacular views and either trade wind cooling or air conditioning units. The cheerful staff at the Grand View delivers a refreshing pitcher of cold water when the guests check in, one of several hospitable touches.

Delicious meals are served at the inn, which specializes in freshly supplied local fish, lobsters, vegetables, and fruit. The dining room in the house, located downstairs, has picture-window views of Great Head Bay and the lush mountains behind. Pretty coral-colored tablecloths, chair pads, and draperies add warmth and cheerfulness, as do the yellow walls and profusion of hanging and potted plants. A built-in hutch adds an antique touch; the room can be a bright breakfast spot or a dazzling nighttime bistro lit up by the lights of the bay. The breakfast menu is quite complete and coffee is served in a handy thermos container for easy guest refills. The honey and jams are delicious, as are the large, warm-from-the-oven breakfast rolls. Lunch might be a shrimp salad or lobster sandwich on the patio or by the pool, and dinner is a choice of tasty local or continental dishes. A comfortable bar with the same great views of the bay is located off the side veranda and features a piano for informal entertainment.

To the back of the house is the pool, nearly suspended over the ocean just below. Swimmers can relax at the swim-up bar with drinks and survey nearby Young Island or lounge on the comfortable pool furniture. A grassy path lined with a mini-botanical garden of flowering tropical vegetation leads to the lower acreage of the estate, as well as to the inn's small private beach. This park-like area of grass and palms makes for leisurely strolling and serene pastoral views.

❋

The Heron Hotel
Bay Street, P.O. Box 226, Kingstown, St. Vincent, West Indies

Phone: (809) 457–1631
Key: Inn; 15 units; Inexpensive CP year-round; VI, MC, AE.
Location: In town; 4 mi. to beach; 2 mi. to airport.

The second-story Heron Hotel once topped an estate's plantation warehouse and was originally used as a lodging facility for the estate's owners and managers when they made trips from their northern St. Vincent plantation into town. The Georgian building, whose exact date of construction is unknown, is remarkably the same today except for the addition of many modern-day comforts, including private baths, air conditioning, and telephones.

The intimate hotel is nestled right downtown, opposite the waterfront and next to the shopping district. A small river that flows through Kingstown and past the side-rear of the hotel is responsible for the inn's name. The heron no longer resides in the river, but the hotel is in its thirty-second year of operation.

The upstairs entry of the hotel contains the reception desk, a bookcase brimming with readables, and the dining area where all three meals are served. Breakfast and dinner are both included in the stay at this inn; breakfast is often shared with local people who enjoy the plentiful breakfast fare of fruit juice and fruit, toast with marmalade, and eggs. The hearty dinner includes soup, a meat entree, vegetables, dessert, and coffee. All of this is served in the cheery ambience of homey flowered valances, lots of green plants, and fresh flowers from the garden. A tiny bar here serves various hard and soft drinks, which can be enjoyed in the guest lounge nearby.

Just beyond the reception area is the spacious and airy guest lounge with television, vaulted ceilings, and cane and rattan furniture outfitted with brightly colored pillows. A second guest retreat can be found on the sunporch toward the rear of the building. This cozy spot looks over the South River beyond the back door of the porch and boasts comfortable chairs and a greenhouse of plants.

All of the guestrooms at the Heron are different in both size and decor; all wrap around the sides of the building with various views of town and the waterfront. All of the guest lodgings boast built-in vanities. Most of the rooms convey an airy feel, with walls washed in pastel shades and homey calico window valances and lace curtains. When not in use, the doors to the rooms are left open to keep them very fresh. Room #15 at the inn boasts a large sitting area, two beds, and curtains in an orange and gold calico print that gives the spacious room a comfortable, home-like feel.

The Heron Hotel is a simple inn that has been granting true "home away from home" hospitality and good West Indian cooking for more than a quarter of a century in a structure designed to do just that. Its charm is very local and represents a true bargain amid warmth and basic comforts.

✳

Kingstown Park Guest House
P.O. Box 41, St. Vincent, West Indies

Phone: (809) 456–1532
Key: Guest house; 22 units; Inexpensive year-round EP; No credit cards.
Location: Near town; 3 mi. to beach; 2^1/$_2$ mi. to airport.

On a hilltop overlooking the town of Kingstown and granting spectacular views of the sea and emerald-green mountains is this personally run guest house owned by Miss Nesta Paynter, a retired St. Vincent government worker and all-around interesting person. At the core of the guest lodgings is the main house, a century-old plantation-style structure that was once a prestigious family home. Ten guestrooms and the dining room are located in the antique home, and the remainder of the guest accommodations are found in the newer buildings of brick and stone on the property.

The gray wooden siding of the main house is a bit frayed, but in keeping with the antique interiors. The guest enters through the parlor brimming with antiques, polished wooden floors, curios, and organdy curtains. A high cathedral ceiling has been painted white, and an elegant crystal chandelier hangs from its center. The walls are covered in interesting old photographs that were taken by none other than the innkeeper herself, who not known to many, was the first lady photographer on the island. The photos were meticulously hand-painted by Miss Paynter.

All of the guestrooms in the main house are furnished with a sprinkling of antiques. All of the guestrooms, some with shared bath, are airy and clean with an emphasis on comfort, rather than fanciness. Groups are welcome at the guest house and a common sight; the guest house receives its share of return clientele who enjoy the quaintness and budget accommodations.

The dining room is located downstairs in the main house and retains the old stone walls and beamed ceilings of the home; seating is provided at antique tables and chairs. This turn-of-the-century room leads to a pleasant backyard patio with a small, manicured garden and inspiring views as far as you can see. Although situated in a residential area, the guest house is just a five-minute walk from town.

✳

Also on the Island

The Umbrella Beach Hotel
Box 530, St. Vincent, West Indies

Phone: (809) 458–4651

Located on "The Strip" across from Young Island, The Umbrella Beach Hotel is a simple, old Caribbean-style hotel and a great bargain. There are ten units, each with small kitchens and porches overlooking the bay. Rates are inexpensive EP year round.

✳

The Grenadines

You can reach some of the Grenadine islands by air, but the least expensive means is by boat. Mail, cargo, and passenger boats travel among the islands, but check schedules carefully. Boats tend to be slow and do not run every day of the week.

Young Island in the Grenadines is just 200 yards off St. Vincent and can be reached easily via a ferry that resembles a small, rustic *African Queen* and that runs constantly between the two islands, taking about five minutes. The 25-acre, mountain island provides visitors with breathtaking views, tropical foliage, and an eighteenth-century fort sculpted from an enormous rock, 200 feet above the sea. One resort, the Young Island Resort, comprises the entire sleepy island and has a low-key bar and restaurant and cottages.

Bequia lies ten miles south of St. Vincent and, measuring seven miles square, is the largest of the Grenadines. This sea-oriented island is reached only by boat and is a favorite anchoring spot. A ferry departs daily at noon from St. Vincent and begins the return trip the following morning at six. Its gold sand beaches and quiet coves are excellent for sailing, scuba, and snorkeling. The age-old traditions of boat-building, whaling, and fishing are the main concerns of the tiny island. The waterfront town of Port Elizabeth offers bars, restaurants, and small shops.

Mustique is a privately owned, 2^1/$_2$-mile gem. Soft green hills, white sand, and turquoise waters attract the elite. Cotton House, an eighteenth-century converted plantation house, is the only resort there and offers magnificent and secluded accommodations that cater to the jet-set.

Other principal islands in the Grenadines include Canouan, boasting some of the best beaches in the Caribbean; Tobago Cays, with spectacular coral reefs; Mayreau; Union Island; Palm Island; Carriacou, and the southernmost island of Petit St. Vincent.

✳

Frangipani Hotel
P.O. Box 1, Bequia, St. Vincent and The Grenadines, West Indies

Phone: (809) 458–3255
Key: Inn; 15 units; Moderate/Inexpensive EP; VI, MC, AE.
Location: On beach; Near town; 12 mi. to airport.

Poised on the shore of Admiralty Bay, the location of this family estate-turned-inn is nearly ideal. It is just a short walk away from the St. Vincent ferry stop in Port Elizabeth and a close jaunt to beautiful

Frangipani Hotel, St. Vincent and The Grenadines

Tony Gibbons Beach and Friendship Bay. The anchorage at Admiralty Bay is considered one of the best in the Caribbean, thus giving this inn world-wide recognition from the yachting set. The grounds of the estate are casual and tranquil, boasting a nice garden and lots of mango, citrus, and papaya trees.

A range of accommodations is available at the Frangipani, all at fairly reasonable rates. The most economy-minded rooms are found upstairs in the main house. These rooms share a bath, but each has its own wash-basin/vanity area for convenience. The decor is simpler here, but the guestrooms carry a homestyle charm not found in the newer cottages. The stone-and-timber cottages all have private, spacious bathrooms, a dressing room, and a large sundeck with views of the ocean. These very private facilities are decorated attractively with ceramic tile floors, wooden louvered doors, and modern furnishings.

The restaurant of the inn overlooks the yacht anchorage and is the meeting spot for guests, locals, and visiting yachtsmen. All three meals are offered here, along with delicious rum punches and pina coladas made from fresh fruit juices. The reasonably priced menu concentrates on locally produced vegetables, fruit, fish, and lobster provided by the island's fishermen. Local musicians liven up the spot once or twice a week, and the Thursday night barbecue/buffet with live entertainment is a popular tradition.

The Frangipani now offers a tennis court and is constructing a windsurfing center. The friendly staff, headed by manager Marie

Kingston, is happy to make any arrangements for charter yachting, snorkeling, windsurfing, or tennis.
Note: The inn is closed in September.

✳

Friendship Bay Hotel
P.O. Box 9, Bequia, St. Vincent and The Grenadines, West Indies

Phone: (809) 458–3222
Key: Inn; 27 units; Expensive/Inexpensive CP; MC, VI, AE.
Location: On beach; 1 mi. to town; 5 mi. to airport (Mustique).

This small, family-run inn is located on a tropically lush, twelve-acre estate on a pretty stretch of beach. The thirty-year-old hostelry was recently purchased by Lars and Margit Abrahamson, a Swedish couple who are in the process of upgrading all the guestrooms and public rooms.

The resort offers ten superior beach cottages, five hillside cottages, and twelve standard rooms, each with private balcony and bath. All of the accommodations are newly redecorated, with ceiling fans in each unit and views of the sea from every room. Room decor includes straw floor mats, rattan seating, brightly-printed bedspreads and draperies, and attractive island wall hangings. At the time of this writing, a suite was under construction.

Breakfast is included in your stay at Friendship Bay, and lunch is offered at both the beach bar and in the dining room. Dinners, served in the recently redecorated dining room with Spanish tile floors, lots of fresh plants, and romantic views of the other Grenadine islets, consist mainly of fresh lobster and fish caught daily, along with a selection of international dishes.

Guests may want to live in their swimsuits most of the time at this causal inn on a mile-long, sandy beach. Windsurfing, snorkeling, swim rafts, parasailing, and speedboat and yachting excursions to other islets are all available. Guests may also enjoy tennis, table tennis, and an attractive guest lounge with crystal chandelier, reading material, and a large handmade tapestry depicting life in Bequia.

✳

Cotton House Hotel
Mustique, St. Vincent and The Grenadines, West Indies

Phone: (809) 456–4777
Representative: Ralph Locke Islands

This privately owned island, measuring three miles by one-and-a-half miles, has just one elite resort, the Cotton House Hotel. The eighteenth-century plantation house boasts public rooms decorated in exquisite antiques and serves afternoon tea on the veranda. The guest quarters include stone villas and cottages, also tastefully decorated. The once private club opened to the public several years ago and offers, along with seclusion, a hilltop swimming pool, tennis, horseback riding, and all water sports on its beautiful beaches.

Palm Island Beach Club
Palm Island, St. Vincent and The Grenadines, West Indies

Phone: (809) 458–8824; (800) 776–PALM

You won't be on this island for more than five minutes and you'll know all about "Coconut Johnny." If you want to acquaint yourself with him sooner, read his book, *Desperate Voyage,* which tells his story (John Caldwell's story) of sailing around the world and landing on Palm Island about twenty-five years ago. When he arrived, he planted thousands of palm trees and got a ninety-nine-year lease on the island. Now in his seventies, he's still there, taking care of everything and keeping everybody happy. There are a total of twenty-four rooms in twelve half-stone, half-hardwood bungalows. Each is kept cool by sea breezes that waft in through wooden-slat vertical blinds. On the island, there are five white-sand beaches, a paddle tennis court, and "Highway 90," Johnny's own fitness trail. Rates are deluxe AP year-round.

Petit St. Vincent Resort
Petit St. Vincent, St. Vincent and The Grenadines,
West Indies

Phone: (809) 458–8801; (800) 654–9326

PSV, as those in the know call it, feels like a country club—and then some. It's an ultra-private 113-acre island where the forty-odd guests stay in cottages, all with separate sitting rooms and patios or terraces, and are treated with great care. There's plenty of beach (studded with hammocks), a tennis court with lights, a croquet lawn, table tennis, fitness trail, and foot path up to 275-foot Mount Marni, where the view is well worth it. Rates are deluxe AP, year-round.

Spring on Bequia
Bequia, St. Vincent and The Grenadines, West Indies

Phone: (809) 458–3414

Set off in its own little world in the hills is Spring on Bequia. It is a 250-year-old plantation with ten guest rooms (all refurbished in recent years). Four are in the main lodge, while two are in hillside cottages. The dining room is a wonderful open-air room where many a memorable meal is had. There is a beautiful slice of beach about ten minutes (by foot) away, a pool, one tennis court, and hiking and biking trails.

Young Island Resort
P.O. Box 211, Young Island, St. Vincent, West Indies

Phone: (809) 458–4826
Representative: Ralph Locke Islands

Just 200 yards off St. Vincent is this land with one resort, reached by day and night by a rapid and complimentary ferry ride. The island, consisting of twenty-five acres of tropical flora, has twenty-nine cottages—twenty-four superior, two deluxe, and three luxury suites—sprinkled around the dense hillsides and on the beaches. A saltwater pool, tennis courts, turtle ponds, two forty-four-foot yachts, and very relaxing thatched outdoor bar and dining areas also make up this peaceful resort.

✳

Grenada

Grenada, referred to as the "Isle of Spice," is one of the only spice-producing areas in the Western Hemisphere. The 133-square-mile Grenada includes the two islets, Carriacou and Petit Martinique. Grenada, twelve miles wide and twenty-one miles long, lies 100 miles north of Venezuela and 12 degrees north of the equator.

A new international airport has recently opened on the island at Point Salines, allowing for regularly scheduled, direct flights into the island. Major cruise ships pull into the port at St. Georges as well. Proof of citizenship is required of U.S. citizens, and a small departure tax is charged. Both taxis and self-drive cars are available for touring; local buses operate to some parts of the island.

During the dynastic wars of the eighteenth century, Grenada changed hands several times between the British and French, finally being ceded to the British in 1783. The country became independent in 1974, and a coup of the People's Revolutionary Government took over the government until October 1983. Since the well-known "invasion of Grenada," the island has bounced back and tourists are welcome more than ever.

No matter how far inland you travel you are never more than $6^{1}/_{2}$ miles from one of the forty-five beautiful beaches of Grenada. Its narrow roads wind through foliage-covered mountains with bamboo trees, ferns, and cocoa and banana trees, as well as through farming towns and fishing villages.

Grenville, the second largest city in Grenada, is the locale of the vegetable market and the spice factory, where visitors may watch nutmeg, cocoa, and mace being prepared for export. Saturday is the colorful market day here, when Grenadians do their own marketing. Weavers display hats, baskets, bags, and placemats made from palm fronds.

Sauteurs, on the northernmost tip of Grenada, is the site of the great cliff where the Caribs leapt to their deaths rather than be captured by the French. Levera Beach nearby is a large deserted beach, ringed by sea grapes and palm trees.

The Grand Etang District, with lush mountains and tropical forest, is highlighted by the Annandale Falls and a profusion of orchids, armadillos, and monkeys.

Dougaldston Estate in the market town of Gouyave is another spice factory where various spices are sorted by hand. Tours of the process and storage areas, as well as fresh samples, await the visitor here. Fifteen minutes from the estate is Concord Falls and nearby Betty Mascoll's Plantation, a seventy-seven-year-old plantation home built of hand-chiseled colored stones and mortared with lime and molasses. Visitors may have lunch amid the family antiques.

St. Georges, Grenada's capital city and major port, is a picturesque town of pastel buildings and red tile roofs. The Carenage is the center of activity in town; fishing boats with weekly loading on Tuesdays depart with crates and bags of fruit and vegetables bound for Trinidad. Various shops here display and sell spice- and flower-related goods: perfumes, shampoo, lotions, potpourri, teas, etc. The Grenada National Museum is set in the foundations of an old French army barracks and prison built in St. Georges in 1704. The newest addition to the town is the Marryshow Folk Theatre—Grenada's first cultural center. Plays, West Indian dance, music, and poetry readings are featured in this former home of the West Indian patriot, T. Albert Marryshow. Several forts surround the city, which also boasts a zoo and botanical garden.

Carriacou, Grenada's sister island and one of its island dependencies, is thirteen miles square, with rolling hills and white sand beaches. It is actually the largest of The Grenadines and is a favorite stop for yachtsmen. The main streets of the island run parallel to the beach; its pier is the site of most of the activity. Visitors may tour on foot or by car. A side trip to the town of Windward is interesting because of its villagers of Scottish descent who still build wooden schooners. To reach Carriacou, sixteen miles north of Grenada, you may take a daily flight from Grenada or rent a yacht. Organized tours to the island are also available.

For additional information on Grenada contact:

Grenada Tourist Board
820 Second Avenue, 9D
New York, NY 10017
(212) 687–9554

❋

Secret Harbour Hotel
P.O. Box 11, St. George's, Grenada, West Indies

Phone: (809) 440–4439
Key: Inn; 20 units; Deluxe/Deluxe EP; AE, VI, MC.
Location: On beach; 5 mi. to town; 30 mi. to airport.

This Mediterranean-looking complex that rambles through the lush bougainvillea-filled hillside to the sea is a dream-come-true—at least for owner and creator Barbara Stevens. The ex-accountant from Britain left "it all" to find the perfect spot for her luxurious inn, and this elegant site overlooking Hartman Bay on the south coast was to be the setting.

Red-tiled roofs, white arches, and terraces dominate the exterior architecture of the inn, while antiques, stained glass, colorful Italian tile, and color-coordinated furnishings dominate the interiors. The overall effect is elegant and special. The lobby, lounge, and restaurant are located at the very top of the hill and feature heavy beamed ceilings and wrought-iron light fixtures. Breakfast and dinner are served in the tasteful surroundings.

The luxurious suites are located in cottages close to the beach and feature double mahogany four-poster beds covered in designer-coordinated fabrics in each guest accommodation. Each spacious guest suite boasts a sprinkling of choice antiques that have been lovingly restored, a dressing room, living room area, and private patio, as well as an incredible bathroom with a sunken tub lined in Italian tile. Everything coordinates nicely, including the towels, and potted plants add warmth and flair.

From the private cottages guests may climb a few steps up the lush hillside to the free-form swimming pool, lined in the same eye-appealing tilework, and to the tennis court, or take a few frangipani- and palm-lined steps down to the sandy beach with convenient bar.

✺

Also on the Island

Calabash
P.O. Box 382, St. George's, Grenada, West Indies

Phone: (809) 444–4334
Representative: International Travel & Resorts, Inc.

Situated on Prickly Bay on eight acres of tropical grounds is this hospitable inn, named after a popular Caribbean gourd-like fruit. Twenty-two suites are located in the ten cottages around the grounds and close to the beach, each with its own bathroom, sitting area, kitchenette, and porch. The contemporary structures of wood and stucco with louvered windows are pleasant and come with a breakfast maid who will cheerfully serve you the morning fare on your patio, in the sitting area, or even in bed. One guest accommodation boasts a private swimming pool. Delicious island-food lunches and dinners are served in the natural stone pavilion covered in aromatic tropical vines. The sheltered water and powdery sand beach make for good swimming, snorkeling, and sunbathing activities. Winter MAP rates are deluxe, with off-season rates dropping to expensive on the CP.

Spice Island Inn
P.O. Box 6, St. George's, Grenada, West Indies

Phone: (809) 444–4258
Representative: International Travel & Resorts, Inc.

This small hotel offers accommodations directly on renowned Grand Anse Beach. There are fifty-six suites, each with a whirlpool and/or Jacuzzi, or a private swimming pool inside a walled garden. All of the suites are comfortably and nicely furnished with a maximum of privacy. The main house of the inn has a dining area and dancing, and an outside patio provides meals in a tropical setting. Weekly, local entertainment is provided, and a boutique is located on the grounds. The year-round stay is deluxe MAP.

✳

St. Lucia

Like Dominica, St. Lucia is green and mountainous. Its highest peak, Mount Gimie, is 3,117 feet. On the island, often identified by its twin green volcanic mountains, are many species of exotic flowers and plants, such as orchids and anthuriums that grow wild in the dense rain forests. In contrast, the southern portion of St. Lucia is characterized by flatter, somewhat hilly land. Living only on St. Lucia is the beautiful Amazon Versicolor Parrot.

The twenty-seven-mile-long by fourteen-mile-wide island was purchased by the French India Company in 1650. The following 150 years saw it change hands fourteen times between the English and French until being ceded to the British in 1814. St. Lucia (pronounced Loosha) obtained its independence from Britain in 1979 and is now a member of the Commonwealth of Nations.

English is the official language of the island, but due to the French historical influence, most of the 152,000 inhabitants speak a French Creole as well.

International non-stop airlines fly into the island and inter-island airlines and on-island charters are available. Identification in the form of a passport, birth certificate, or voter registration card is required for U.S. citizens, and a departure tax is levied upon leaving. There is no well organized public bus system on the island, but taxis with drivers trained in a special sightseeing program, as well as car rentals, are readily available. A temporary driver's license is required, and remember to drive on the left side of the road. Tour operators offer a variety of tours, ranging from on-island plantation, village, and volcano excursions to yachting cruises to nearby islands.

Temperatures on St. Lucia are in the mid-80s year-round with a rainy season August through September. The rains are brief, leaving sunny skies most of the day.

Sightseeing around St. Lucia is sure to include several banana plantations. Bananas are the leading export and the plantations a primary island attraction. The Pitons are the towering, ½-mile-high volcanic mountains that challenge mountain climbers. Soufriere, a scenic fishing village, makes a good base for exploring the Pitons and the sulphur baths once praised by King Louis XVI. The visitor will also find near here Mt. Soufriere, a "drive-in" volcano where cars actually may drive into the ancient crater, allowing passengers to walk about the sulphur springs and pools.

Yachtsmen from around the world congregate at the anchorage town of Marigot Bay, locale of some of the filming of Dr. Doolittle and dotted with fine restaurants. Castries, St. Lucia's capital, is also a favorite port for the yachting set and is known for its colorful Saturday morning street markets, shops, and restaurants. St. Lucia is best known for its cane furnishings and batik on plentiful display here. Castries is a newer town with modern concrete buildings that have replaced most of the French colonial or Victorian structures lost by fires. Still intact, however, are the Government House and a cathedral. Mourne Fortune, or "Hill of Good Fortune," changed hands repeatedly between the French and English and is now an exceptional location to view sunsets over the Castries Harbor.

Pigeon Point is really an island that is connected by a manmade causeway to St. Lucia. It was historically a pirate retreat and site of British forts, the ruins of which are still present. Its white, sandy beaches make it a popular picnic and swimming spot. The beaches of St. Lucia offer not only white sand but also unique pearl-gray sand shores, along with superb sailing and every type of water sport. Glass-bottomed boat trips allow glimpses of the underwater sealife through the clear water below.

Dining in St. Lucia is a blend of French, English, German, and American, as well as creole cuisine. Special food offerings include pumpkin souffle and lobster creole. The nightlife here is relaxed and highlighted by steel bands that perform folk, calypso, and reggae.

For additional information on St. Lucia contact:

St. Lucia Tourist Office
820 Second Avenue
New York, NY 10017
(212) 867–2950

✳

Anse Chastanet
P.O. Box 7000, Soufriere, St. Lucia, West Indies

Phone: (809) 455–7355
Representative: Ralph Locke Islands
Key: Inn; 48 units; Deluxe/Moderate EP; AE, DC, VI, MC.
Location: On beach; 2 mi. to town; 45 mi. to airport.

Rising up from the gray-sand beach of Anse Chastanet is a hillside lushly blanketed in hibiscus, bougainvillea, and tropical greenery, with an occasional whitewashed bungalow peeking out to share the landscape. Anse Chastanet is made up of fourteen charming octagonal cottages, a selection of hillside suites and rooms, beachside suites (six with plunge pools), as well as a main house at the top of the hill, a beachside restaurant and bar, and a few villas that are really houses for rent.

This peaceful retreat offers guest accommodations with inspiring views of the Pitons, the island's spectacular twin peaks, and the hillsides

07-12-97

•4•   0002

1   10•00 11
1   4•00 11
                    0•98 11
                   14•98 11
                   20•00 A
                    5•02 0

          002

19•59   119

from their wrap-around terraces. The pleasant but simple interiors include color-coordinated bedspreads and draperies and furniture of locally crafted wood, and each unit has a private, tiled bath and overhead fan.

Over 100 steps lead from the sand to the main building of the inn, with impressive views and rest-stops along the way. Delicious local dishes are served in the main house dining area and at the palm-lined beach restaurant with thatched bar. Fresh fish is a specialty, often with the daily catch arriving by fishing boat directly at the beach below. All three meals are offered.

The ¹/₄-mile-long beach provides excellent snorkeling and scuba, and the courteous, helpful staff will assist with any vacation details.

✳

Dominica

Dominica, called the "nature island of the Caribbean," is characterized by towering mountains and crisscrossing rivers, lush green valleys, fields of broadleafed bananas, cocoa and lime trees, and abundant tropical foliage. In fact, the island is home to over 135 species of local birds, including the Imperial Parrot and the Red-Necked Parrot, which are found only in Dominica.

Discovered by Columbus in 1493, Dominica was British from 1805 and self-governing since 1967. English is the official language of the 94,000 population, but a French patois is common as well.

Dominica is reached by connecting flights on local airlines north from Antigua or Guadeloupe and south from Martinique or Barbados. Proof of citizenship is required for U.S. citizens, and a nominal airport departure tax is collected upon leaving the island. Getting around Dominica is best done by taxi with government-regulated rates for sightseeing, or with one of the tour companies that offer safaris, boat trips, hiking guides, and more. Jeeps may be rented at some of the hotels, but are not recommended due to poor roads and general driving conditions. If you do rent a vehicle, a license fee is charged.

The daytime temperature of Dominica averages between 70 and 80 degrees with cooler nights, especially in the mountain areas. Brief showers that keep the vegetation lush can come any time of the year, but mainly June through October.

Proof that nature is Dominica's main offering is even evident in the capital city of Roseau on the calm leeward coast. Rivers gurgle through the quiet town that offers little nightlife and a small amount of shopping. The Saturday market held in the square is a time to peruse the grass rugs made in Roseau, as well as Carib baskets and various bamboo, coconut, and "Foujere" seashell handcrafts.

The town of Portsmouth boasts the best and most attractive harbor on the island. Close to here is the Indian River, which can be explored by canoe, winding through the ancient mangrove trees that line the banks. Two miles north of the harbor town are the twin peaks of the Cabrits, upon which stand the remains of an eighteenth-century garrison with over 200 acres filled with major structures, lookouts, and barracks. The Portsmouth Harbour and Douglas Bay are also popular areas for scuba, sailing, windsurfing, and waterskiing.

Safari trips can be arranged from Portsmouth across Dominica to explore the Tropical Rain Forest, the sulphur springs, waterfalls, the Boiling Lake, Freshwater Lakes, the Carib Indian Reservation, and the Emerald Pool. The Emerald Pool in the Morne Trois Pitons National Park is reached by a one-half-mile loop trail canopied by trees and plants. The Middleham Trails here take the hiker through a true rain forest to a viewpoint overlooking one of Dominica's tallest waterfalls, Middleham Fall. Boiling Lake in the Pitons Park is five miles east of Roseau and is the world's second largest boiling lake. The temperature along the edges ranges from 180 to 197 degrees. This cauldron of bubbling, greyish-blue water is usually enveloped in a cloud of vapor and is believed to be the result of a crack through which gases escape from the molten lava below the earth.

For additional information on Dominica contact:

Caribbean Tourism Organization
20 East 46th Street
New York, NY 10017
(212) 682–0435

*

Papillote Wilderness Retreat
P.O. Box 67, Roseau, Dominica, West Indies

Phone: (809) 448–2287
Key: Inn; 10 units; Inexpensive EP year-round; AE, MC, VI, DC.
Location: In forest; 4 mi. to town; 8 mi. or 41 mi. to airports.

This "little butterfly," as its name translates, is appropriately a part of the surrounding natural environment. Located in a small rain forest in the Papillote Forest, this secluded inn offers a garden setting of begonias, hibiscus, bromeliads, and ferns among waterfalls, rivers, and hot springs. Owners and managers Cuthbert and Anne Jean-Baptiste are pleased to lead guests to the best in natural delights the tiny forest has to offer.

The Papillote offers ten comfortably furnished guestrooms and the architecture is basically West Indian, with large, airy verandas.

The veranda restaurant, overlooking breadfruit trees and ferns, has peaceful tropical garden and waterfall views and serves superb natural and vegetarian cuisine. The gourmet health food includes freshly caught fish, salads punctuated with exotic fruit and vegetables from the garden, homemade breads, and herb tea fresh from the herbal garden. Breakfast here might start with a banana or papaya plucked from a tree outside your window.

The inn is a popular starting point for nature walks, and guests may also delight in an invigorating river swim under a secluded waterfall or a soak in a natural hot mineral bath. The innkeepers will arrange day tours and guided nature walks to rare and unusual places on request in this unique, "organic" wilderness retreat.

Note: Guests arriving at the island's Canefield airport rather than Melville Hall's airport will save over thirty miles in travel to reach the inn.

✳

Reigate Hall Hotel
Reigate, Dominica, West Indies

Phone: (809) 448–4031
Key: Inn; 17 units; Inexpensive EP year-round; AE, MC, VI.
Location: 3 mi. to beach; 1 mi. to town; 3 mi. to airport.

Set in the hills above Roseau, Reigate Hall Hotel is a restored estate house-turned-inn.

Reigate Hall has seventeen guest accommodations, all with private, well appointed baths. The guestrooms feature 150-year-old wooden beams, balconies with bay views, air conditioning, and some four-posters and televisions.

Both lunch and dinner are served in the "hanging" restaurant with a functional waterwheel and wood and stone interiors. Unusual for a hotel of this size, Reigate Hall offers guests twenty-four-hour room service.

Guests have plenty to do at the inn, including a swimming pool, tennis court, sauna, gameroom, and gymnasium. The inn's two bars are located poolside and in the lounge.

✻

Also on the Island

Springfield Plantation
P.O. Box 41, Roseau, Dominica, West Indies

Phone: (809) 445–1401

This Victorian plantation house with outbuildings has spectacular views of the countryside from its 1,200-foot elevation just a few miles from the National Park entrance. The turn-of-the-century house is furnished in some homey antiques and has seven pleasant guestrooms. Several cottages and apartments on the grounds can also be rented for extended stays with monthly rates available. The picturesque inn serves good island food and offers a river-fed pool to guests. Overnight rates are moderate year-round, and include breakfast and dinner. The plantation is about six miles from town and three miles from the Cane-field airport.

Barbados

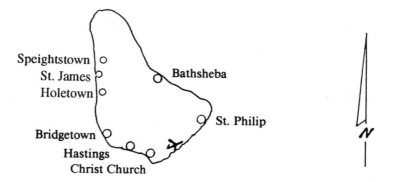

Speightstown
St. James
Holetown
Bathsheba
St. Philip
Bridgetown
Hastings
Christ Church

N

One of the most wonderful things about Barbados is that it still has that island feeling most people look for in a Caribbean vacation. "Condominiumitis" hasn't hit, prices haven't soared to unforgivable heights, and the local residents—known as Bajans—genuinely welcome visitors. On top of that, Barbados has an island cuisine of its own, some fine inns and hotels, and some of the Caribbean's most spectacular scenery. Situated in the far eastern Caribbean, it's blessed with a west coast that's lapped by gentle washes of silky blue sea and a rugged east coast lined with cliffs that drop precipitously into the Atlantic Ocean.

While most Caribbean islands are volcanic, 166-square-mile Barbados is made of coral; the 60,000-year-old coral base of the island acts as a natural purification system, providing some of the purest water in the world. Its mainly flat and open topography also boasts gently rolling hills and has accounted for the island's history of prosperous sugar production. The influence of Dutch traders is present today in the abandoned windmills that grace the valleys, once used to power the first sugar factories.

For 350 years, this small island lived and flourished under the British crown. In 1966 it became a fully independent Commonwealth nation. Today, traces of the mother country are everywhere. In Bridgetown, a bronze statue of Lord Nelson stands in Trafalgar Square, the heart of the city. The House of Assembly, north of the square, has stained glass windows representing the English monarchs. You can detect a bit of old Shakespearean English in the modern Barbadian dialect (words like yonder are commonly used). Many of the hotels—and some restaurants—serve afternoon tea.

Many airlines fly directly into Barbados, as well as connect with other islands in the Caribbean. The airport has the longest runway in the area and is capable of accommodating the largest of jets. U.S. citizens need only identification (valid passport, original birth certificate, or voter's registration card) and a return ticket for entry. At departure, a nominal departure tax is collected unless the visit is less than twenty-four hours.

The Barbados dollar is the currency. Pegged to the U.S. dollar, it is equal to 50 U.S. cents. Many of the stores and restaurants will accept American dollars, major credit cards, and traveler's checks as well. Electricity on the island is fairly reliable and operates on North American standards. The language of Barbados is English, but with a distinctive Creole variation referred to as a Bajan dialect. The island is on Atlantic Standard Time all year and shares the same time as the East Coast during Eastern Daylight Saving months.

Barbados enjoys warm, sunny days, cooled by constant sea breezes year-round. The winter temperature ranges from 70 to 85 degrees; summer ranges from 76 to 87 degrees. Brief showers occur September through November. June through October is the hurricane season, but hurricanes are unusual on the island. The most recent was in August, 1980, but before that the island had not been touched by a hurricane since September, 1955.

Getting around Barbados is easy via taxi, bus, or rental car. Taxis, located at hotels, airport, and important destinations, are not equipped with meters but can be hired by the hour (or any part of) or by the mile. Rental cars (including an open-aired vehicle called a Mini-Moke), scooters, and bicycles are available by the day or week; driving is on the left side of the road. Those opting for rental car transportation should note that the airport rental car agencies often close in late evening. Also, the roads around the countryside tend to be bumpy and curvy, not always well marked and populated by fast local drivers who do not adhere to the twenty- to thirty-mile-per-hour speed limits. Drivers must obtain a Barbados driver's license, which is available simply by showing a U.S. license at the car-rental agency. The cost is roughly $5 U.S. Bus service on the island is comprehensive, offering blue Transport Board buses as well as colorful mini-buses on scheduled routes, and fares are very reasonable. Both stop at the red-and-white bus stop markers. Local tour operators offering specialized island tours are well-represented.

Barbados has a population of approximately 259,000 persons, with around 98,000 in the capital, Bridgetown. Bridgetown is an exuberant little city with streets always busy with shoppers, tourists, local business people, and vendors selling everything from slices of freshly chopped coconut to plastic sandals. The Board of Tourism has designed a terrific walking tour and map that you can pick up free at any of the tourist booths. Among the main attractions in town are Trafalgar Square, with its Nelson Statue and Victorian Public Buildings (where the Assembly and Legislative Council meet), the Old Synagogue (1654), St. Michael's Cathedral (George Washington supposedly worshipped here in 1751), and the Careenage area (an inlet bustling with colorful fishing boats and yachts). There are also plenty of shops at Pelican Village, which is a shopping center geared for tourists on the edge of town.

From Bridgetown, it's a short bus or taxi ride to the Garrison Savannah, which was the training ground for British soldiers stationed in Barbados during the 1960s and is now the site of major sporting and ceremonial events. It's also home to the Barbados Museum, a conscientiously assembled collection of Barbadian artworks, antiques, and arti-facts.

Those interested in native flora will want to visit Barbados' many botanical sites, including Welchman's Hall Gully, a botanical garden with exotic fruit and spice trees; Turner's Hall Woods, forty-five acres of the only virgin forest on the island; the Flower Forest, fifty acres of tropical blossoms; the Animal Flower Cave, natural grottoes and sea pools filled with anemones; and Andromeda Gardens, with its terraced gardens of exotic and colorful plants.

Several old fishing villages set in natural beauty and displaying colo-nial period architecture can be found around the shoreline of Barbados. Reminders of sugar plantation days are at the Morgan Lewis Mill, a restored Dutch sugar cane planter windmill open to the public in St. Andrews. Other sights worth visiting include the Newcastle Coral Stone Gates from the movie *Island in the Sun* and commanding views of the magnificent east coast beaches. Spectacular views are also had from Cherry Tree Hill, flanked by casuarina and mahogany trees. Nearby is one of the island's most popular attractions: The Barbados Wildlife Reserve, where turtles, peacocks, green monkeys, and other reptiles, birds, and animals wander freely (unfortunately, the monkeys have fig-ured out a way to get out, but they do return at mealtimes). The East Coast Road through St. Joseph to Bathsheba is a popular driving tour with a look at the dramatic surf, treacherous reefs, and the charming sea-side village of Bathsheba, reminiscent of England's rocky coastal towns.

A special excursion to Harrison's Cave near Welchman's Hall Gully goes past historic homes, churches, and fields of sugar cane. The tour of the caves begins with a slide show, then entails a guided tram ride into the cavern area with its bubbling streams, waterfalls, and deep pools. The public is also guided on a walk beside a forty-foot-high waterfall during the tour.

Historic sightseeing around Barbados includes visit to many old churches and institutions, including St. John's Parish and Codrington Theological College, which was built in 1702 and is the oldest institu-tion of higher learning in the Western Hemisphere. Quite notable is the antique woodwork that graces the college's church. Historic touring should also include Holetown, where the British first landed, and Gun Hill, a nineteenth-century convalescent center for British West Indies troops and the location of a giant 1868 white coral-stone-carved lion. Four especially worthwhile houses to visit are St. Nicholas Abbey (a Jacobean great house), Villa Nova (a beautiful mansion poised on a hilltop), Francia House (a traditional plantation house), and Sunbury Plantation House (a 1660 planter's house).

Ample sporting facilities exist in Barbados. The coral reefs to the south and east offer beauty and a wide range of marine life for scuba, skin divers, and spear fishermen. Two sunken wrecks are popular exploration spots. Deep-sea fishing in the north and south includes catches of blue marlin, dolphin (the fish), wahoo, tuna, and sailfish. Yachting, surfing, para sailing, and windsurfing are popular water activities as well.

The national sport of Barbados is cricket, but soccer, horse racing, polo, golf, and tennis are well represented. Several riding stables are on the island.

At night, there's a dazzling array of things to do on Barbados. Two boat companies offer dinner cruises (as well as daytime trips): *The Bajan Queen*, a Mississippi-style riverboat, and *The Jolly Roger*, a sailboat. A dinner show—with lots of singing and dancing—called *1627 And All That* is staged in the courtyard of the Barbados Museum. There are several discos with dancing under the stars as well as movie theaters. And when most places start to yawn, Baxter's Road ("The street that never sleeps") just gets going. Lined with rum shops and quick Bajan food stands, the seedy-looking street is an area of inexhaustible vitality where all strata of society come to socialize through the wee hours.

Several annual festivals showcase the local color and history of the island. The Holetown Festival takes place in February, the Crop-Over Festival is in mid-summer, and the National Festival of Creative Arts spans the months of October through November.

For more information on Barbados contact:

> Barbados Board of Tourism Office
> 800 Second Avenue
> New York, NY 10017
> (800) 221–9831; (212) 986–6516
> *or*
> 3440 Wilshire Blvd., Suite 1215
> Los Angeles, CA 90010
> (800) 221–9831; (213) 380–2198

✳

Bagshot House
St. Lawrence, Christ Church, Barbados, West Indies

Phone: (809) 435–6956
Key: Inn; 16 units; Expensive/Expensive MAP; No credit cards.
Location: On beach; 2 mi. to town; 6 mi. to airport.

This small inn fronts the pink coral sands of the St. Lawrence coast and offers a natural lagoon for swimming. The Bagshot House was the first small modern hotel to be built in Barbados. It was constructed on the site of an old family home also called "Bagshot House" after the town of Bagshot in England.

The contemporary concrete structure with split-level roof has a spacious front courtyard, beach frontage, and a relaxing garden patio. The dining area, guest lounge, and entry are all decorated in pleasant pastel shades with handmade rush carpets, tropical decor, and wrought-iron dining tables and chairs. The sixteen guestrooms all feature private baths and twin beds, radios, telephones, and some boast ocean-view balconies. The guestrooms have pastel color schemes with floral curtains and wall-to-wall carpeting.

Both breakfast and dinner are included in the lodging at this inn; breakfast may be American or European. Dinner is table d'hote, and sandwich and soup lunches are available.

Owner and manager of Bagshot House, in operation for more than thirty-five years, is hospitable Mrs. Eileen Robinson. Mrs. Robinson takes pride in the repeat clientele who come back each year for a stay in this informal and unique setting.

✳

Fairholme Hotel and Apartments
Maxwell, Christ Church, Barbados, West Indies

Phone: (809) 428–9425
Key: Inn; 31 units; Inexpensive/Inexpensive EP; No credit cards.
Location: Across from beach; 6 mi. to town; 5 mi. to airport.

Fairholme Hotel and Apartments, Barbados

The Fairholme is actually a converted plantation house that was once a part of the Old Maxwell Plantation. The area around the hotel is so developed that you would not suspect a plantation had existed in that particular spot—that is, until you walk around the still-tranquil grounds of the hotel or peek inside the 1880 structure itself. The original sugar cane manager's residence with a Mediterranean influence and fancy wrought-iron grillwork has been altered somewhat but still has the hurricane shutters and twelve-inch-thick walls that give away its age.

Accommodations at the Fairholme consist of eleven guestrooms in the old mansion and another twenty apartments that were built in 1974 in a similar Mediterranean-style architecture. The apartments have kitchenettes with all the necessities, private shower baths, twin beds, air conditioning, small private patios, and simple decor with block walls. The mansion's offerings, on the other hand, are all very individual, with rooms located both upstairs and down. All of these rooms have private baths, some with spacious tubs and others with showers; some have sinks in the room as well. Iron headboards, armoires, rattan, and flowered curtains and bedspreads are used throughout to make the mansion guestrooms personally yet simply furnished. All of the thirty-one units at the Fairholme are immaculately maintained.

The guest lounge of the main house has blue commercial-type carpeting and a mixture of antique and 1950s contemporary furnishings. It's not out to win design awards, but does win out on hospitality and comfort. A piano here encourages guests to relax with music, and a small patio off the lounge is the site of romantic evening coffee-sipping.

The dining area of the mansion has red vinyl tile floors and black wrought-iron tables and chairs that blend well with the arches and thick stone walls. A few antique serving buffets add warmth to the room. The menu here includes reasonable breakfast, light lunch, and dinner fare.

The grounds, to the back, are far off the busy road and have a rural and hospitable charm as well. The spacious, grassy area has an abundance of colorful hibiscus in shades of orange, pink, and red; lots of hanging planters and potted flowers and plants; fruit trees with lovely aromas; a medium-size pool; a bar and informal entertainment area; and a welcoming resident cat and dog. Fairholme guests are welcome to use the private beach across the street.

The manager of the Fairholme Hotel is Joyce Noble, a very pleasant, congenial person who believes in giving her guests special attention. The result is that the establishment is not only charming, but gives very personal service. Not surprisingly, the Fairholme has many repeat visitors.

✳

Ginger Bay Beach Club
St. Philip, Barbados, West Indies

Phone: (809) 423–5810
Reservations: (800) 223–9815; (212) 545–8469
Key: Inn; 16 suites; Deluxe/Expensive EP; Credit cards accepted.
Location: On beach; approximately 5 miles to airport.

Magnificently situated on limestone cliffs above the thrashing Atlantic, the Ginger Bay Beach Club is off in a world of its own on Barbados' southeast coast.

Its suites are housed in three two-story villas painted a notice-me pink. All sixteen of them are refreshingly breezy, with terraces or patios (hammocks, too), separate sitting rooms, kitchenettes, and spic-and-span white-tile bathrooms. All have air conditioning and ceiling fans, direct-dial telephones, and radios.

Many guests divide their time between the hotel's pool and the beach. To reach the latter, you climb down through a spectacular natural grotto that looks like something you'd see in Walt Disney World.

On a typical day, the beach itself is the kind most people dream of: The sand looks as thought it were washed in bleach, huge Atlantic waves rush in triumphantly, the sun is startlingly bright, the sky as clear as a window. Swimming and snorkeling are available when the surf is tame enough.

The pool and whirlpool are the focal points of the hotel, along with a kiosk bar and the thatch-roofed restaurant called Ginger's, where all three meals are served. There is one tennis court, lighted for night play. The dinner menu features Bajan specialties such as callalloo, flying fish, and dolphin (the fish).

✳

Kingsley Club
Bathsheba, Barbados, West Indies

Phone: (809) 433–9422 or 433–9558
Key: Historic inn; 8 units; Moderate/Moderate EP; Credit cards accepted.
Location: Across from beach; 12 mi. to airport.

Located in the foothills of Bathsheba, on the east side of the island, the Kingsley Club offers picturesque views of the rugged Atlantic shore-

Kingsley Club, Barbados

line. This stretch of wide and rocky beach that meets with pastoral green hills and trees is reminiscent of English coastal areas and brings a different kind of Caribbean charm to this historic inn.

Built as a plantation family's dwelling in 1800, the inn has a tranquil feel on its lawn-covered hilltop site surrounded by two acres of landscaped gardens and trees. The white structure with green pitched roof and green awnings is neat and unassuming. A flight of stairs leads to the dining area and reception area. The dining room, offering an interior area and a sunporch section with beautiful ocean views, is very charming and renowned for its homemade cuisine. The white wicker chairs and loveseats are covered in quaint Laura Ashley prints of blue, and the white wicker tables boast pretty burgundy and white Laura Ashley print coverings, with contrasting napkins and little bouquets of fresh flowers. The feeling is turn-of-the-century and relaxing, and the establishment's popularity is revealed in the busy luncheon trade that dines on four courses, homemade soup through pie.

An old-fashioned feeling of hospitality is also in the lodging end of the inn. The decor is a blend of simple but clean contemporary and rattan furnishings. The eight guestrooms, located along a long corridor, all have the same spectacular views of famous Cattlewash Beach and similar furnishings. Guest accommodations include four double-bedrooms with private baths, wooden floors with area rugs and tropical print fabrics, three "double-double rooms" with similar furnishings, and one suite with a sitting area. All of the modest but pleasant rooms are air cooled by the ever-present hilltop breezes.

The friendly staff and owners of the Kingsley Club, Loris and Sherry Arevian, make the inn a special place to stay where the guest may enjoy a peaceful getaway and some homestyle dining.

✳

The Ocean View Hotel
Hastings, Barbados, West Indies

Phone: (809) 427–7821
Key: Historic inn; 40 units; Expensive/Moderate EP; Credit cards accepted.
Location: On beach; 2 mi. to town; 8 mi. to airport.

The Ocean View is one of the oldest hotels in Barbados, founded in 1901, and is known for its old world charm and courteous service. It's an elegant pink and white colonial house right on the ocean.

The Ocean View, Barbados

The forty guestrooms at Ocean View are all different, some small and intimate, others spacious and airy. Some of the guest accommodations are furnished in the original mahogany antique beds and armoires, while others are decorated in rattan and island furnishings. All of the guestrooms have private baths, air conditioning, and polished wooden floors. A few of the units offer views of the sea and quaint detailing such as petal design cut-outs over the doorways. The guest accommodations, on the second floor, are reached by a beautiful mahogany staircase off the parlor.

The main parlor offers an attractive assortment of antique furnishings, a stately grandfather clock, fresh floral arrangements, and comfortable seating. The "Crystal Room," named so because of the impressive crystal chandelier hanging from the carved-beam ceiling, has more intimate seating, with pastel print couches, antique tables, and a large formal antique dining room set. Tasteful oil paintings hang throughout the small hotel.

The dining room of the hotel has an almost boat-like feel as it reaches out to the dramatic sea. White tables and chairs and various antique tables and sideboards give the room a period feel, while the white lattice ceiling and arches offer an airy atmosphere. The hotel holds a Sunday Planters' Luncheon Buffet, a hotel tradition for many years, with Bajan specialties, such as flying fish, pepperpot, and callaloo soup. All three meals are offered at the hotel.

Guests here may enjoy a pretty white sand beach or a protected natural coral pool. A cocktail bar with piano offers a relaxing atmosphere adjacent to the restaurant.

To illustrate the personal attention offered by the staff at Ocean View, a few of the regular services include beds turned down at night, shoes shined while you sleep, room service, and gracious table service, such as vegetables passed in elegant silver dishes.

✳

Sandpiper Inn
Holetown, St. James, Barbados, West Indies

Phone: (809) 422–2251
Reservations: (800) 223–1108
Key: Inn; 45 rooms (19 are suites); Deluxe/Expensive MAP; Credit cards accepted.
Location: On beach; approximately 8 mi. to Bridgetown; 10 mi. to airport.

Though "inn" is somewhat of a misnomer considering Sandpiper's growth (in recent years, they've added rooms), it maintains the feeling of a small, feel-right-at-home hostelry.

Guestrooms and suites are roomy, rustic yet chic, and thoughtfully outfitted with paperback books and fresh cut flowers. All are handsomely decorated with rattan furniture, straw mats, and jalousie doors that open onto private terraces or balconies. Many look out on a lushly landscaped courtyard and the pool; some are right smack on the beach. The suites are like little apartments, with a sitting room and kitchen in addition to a bedroom or two.

Meals in the dining room are quite good, including a choice of several Bajan and West Indian dishes as well as Continental favorites. On Wednesday night, a special Bajan buffet—complete with steel band music—is prepared.

There's a Best of Barbados shop on the grounds where you can buy watercolors by local artist Jill Walker, straw work, books, and taped island music. Sports include two hard-surface tennis courts across the street and a busy aquatic center (water skiing, snorkeling, boat rides) run by Rambo-like athletes.

✳

Treasure Beach Hotel
Paynes Bay, St. James, Barbados, West Indies

Phone: (809) 432–1346
Reservations: (800) 223–6510; (212) 832–2272
Key: Inn; 25 suites; Deluxe/Deluxe, MAP optional; Credit cards accepted.
Location: On beach; approximately 7 mi. to Bridgetown; 9 mi. to airport.

A day or two here and you start to feel like family. Treasure Beach is a tiny hotel where the staff makes every effort to call guests by name and fellow guests automatically feel a camaraderie. Many of the guests (who are predominately from Great Britain and in other parts of Europe) have been coming year after year. The hotel is owned—and meticulously maintained—by Tony and Elaine Bowen.

The centerpiece of Treasure Beach is a tempting little pool which is surrounded by jungly vines, plants, and hundreds of fragrant blossoms. It's a peaceful spot where guests sit for hours sipping fruity concoctions while they soak in the whole scene. The hotel is also set right smack dab on the beach, and has the usual array of water sports available, from snorkeling to jet-skiing.

All 25 suites—which are in a two-story horseshoe of villas—are gigantic and open onto terraces or balconies hidden behind tangles of sweet-smelling flowers and leafy tropical plants. Many of them have cathedral ceilings and kitchenettes. The upper level is slightly more private.

The open-aired dining room (where breakfast, lunch, and dinner are served) is quite respected on the island. Meals are beautifully prepared by a young Danish chef who has worked in highly-regarded restaurants in France and England.

Some of the amenities include valet and laundry service, safety deposit boxes, and direct-dial telephones.

Trinidad and Tobago

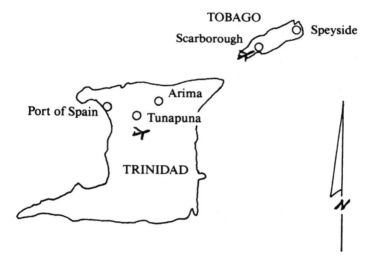

*T*he two-island country of Trinidad and Tobago in the southernmost portion of the Eastern Caribbean offers an incredible mixture of geography, cultures, and abundant wildlife. A wide variety of daily airline flights arrives on the islands from North America, and plentiful inter-island flights connect the islands with other islands in the Caribbean and South America. Cruise ships call regularly here as well. Visitors to Trinidad and Tobago do need a valid passport and an ongoing or return ticket for entry.

Getting around the two islands can be accomplished by buses, which are inexpensive, and by taxis, which are plentiful and marked by an "H" on the license plate. Rental cars are also available, and U.S. visitors may drive up to ninety days on their license. Driving is on the left side of the road.

The monetary unit is the Trinidad and Tobago dollar, but larger hotels will honor credit cards and traveler's checks as well. The electrical current is 115 or 230 volts, so be sure to check before using American appliances. English is the main language of the two islands, but French, Spanish, and even Chinese and Hindi can be heard. Trinidad and Tobago are on Atlantic Standard time all year, which gives them the same time as the East Coast during Daylight Saving months.

The tropical temperatures on Trinidad and Tobago average 74 degrees at night and 84 degrees during the day year-round. Trade winds keep even the warmest days comfortable.

For additional information on Trinidad and Tobago, contact:

Trinidad and Tobago Tourism Authority
25 West 43rd Street, #1508
New York, NY 10036
(212) 719–0504

❋

Trinidad

Roughly rectangular in shape, Trinidad is approximately fifty miles long and thirty-seven miles wide. Its over one million inhabitants create an interesting international ambience, with African, British, Spanish, Portuguese, Chinese, French, and East Indian nationalities all represented on the island.

Christopher Columbus discovered the lush green island with golden sands in 1498 on his third voyage and named it after the three prominent mountain peaks on the southeast coast and after the Holy Trinity. In 1523 the Spanish established their first settlement here as a base for gold expeditions, which also brought England's Sir Walter Raleigh to Trinidad. Raleigh did not find gold, but used the asphalt from Pitch Lake to caulk his ships. Angostura Bitters, Trinidad's contribution to the drinking world, was brought to Trinidad for commercial production, where it is still produced—its formula a guarded family secret.

Port of Spain is both the capital of the Republic of Trinidad and Tobago and the largest city in Trinidad. The city, whose population is a mixture of over forty races, represents a blend of old and new structures—Victorian gingerbread houses nestled among modern skyscrapers. Frederick Street is the main shopping area, with local handicrafts, boutiques, and Oriental bazaars. At the north end of Frederick Street is the National Museum and Art Gallery, with displays of the dazzling Carnival costumes, and nearby are the Botanic Gardens and Emperor Valley Zoo, with tropical plants and local wild animals.

Historic sights around the island include the 1804 Fort George, with its panoramic views; Fort Picton; Gasparee Caves, known for its interesting stalactites and stalagmites; and River Estate, one of the island's greatest sugar cane plantations, which later became a center for agricultural experimentation.

The Queen's Park Savannah, in the foothills of the Northern Range, comprises 200 acres of race course, football, hockey, and cricket areas, along with magnificent tropical trees and plants. The African tulip tree found here is called "the flame of the forest." Near here are elaborate gingerbread-draped mansions, now official residences and offices, and the Queen's Hall, a modern cultural center.

Wildlife abounds in Trinidad; the continental origin from and proximity to South America has resulted in the unusually diverse fauna. The species list includes 108 mammals, 400 birds, fifty-five reptiles, twenty-five amphibians, and 617 butterflies. The Asa Wright Nature Center at Spring Hill Estate was founded to provide a recreation and tropical wildlife study area. Spring Hill is a cocoa-coffee-citrus plantation surrounded by an impressive rain forest. A special Christmas tour of the Center is conducted each year and features an annual Audubon Society Bird Count.

The Caroni Bird Sanctuary, with acres of marshland and mangroves, also has flocks of Scarlet Ibis and is close to Pitch Lake, which produces asphalt for roadmaking exported all over the world. Horlis Reservoir and Cleaver Woods Park near Sangre Grande provide a scenic drive through lush tropical jungle. Northeast from here is beautiful Balandra Bay; south from Sangre Grande is the spectacular Cocal, with miles of coconut trees that canopy the road, which grants views of the ocean to one side and dense, colorful tropical vegetation to the other side. The scenic drive leads to Mayaro Bay, with palm trees, wide sandy beach, and blue-green water.

Nightlife in Trinidad includes plenty of places to dine, drink, listen to steel band and calypso music, and watch limbo dancing. Calypso began in Trinidad and the witty verses can be heard everywhere on the island. Steel bands also originated in Trinidad and Tobago and are capable of playing any style of music. The cuisine on the island is as international as its people—Chinese, Indian, creole, French, Italian, continental, and local dishes. Local specialties include Callaloo soup (a mixture of crabmeat, okra, and dasheen leaves), "pastelles of minced meat" (meat mixed with corn flour and wrapped in banana leaves) and exotic concoctions of rum, the national drink.

Carnival, held each New Year through Ash Wednesday, is called a way of life in Trinidad and Tobago; it combines spectacular colors, costumes, and on-going gaiety. The costumes, music, parades, and gala parties make the event a popular tourist attraction.

❋

Monique's Guest House
114 Saddle Road, Maraval, Trinidad,
West Indies

Phone: (809) 628–3334
Key: Guest house; 11 units; Inexpensive CP year-round; AE.
Location: Near town; 15 mi. to beach; 19 mi. to airport.

Michael and Monica Charbonne have been welcoming guests in their tidy suburban family home in the luxuriant Maraval Valley for over ten years now. The Charbonnes are most hospitable hosts, who make sure "the guest becomes a member of the family upon arrival." They offer eleven simply furnished rooms, all with private baths, to guests. The guestrooms include some with carpeting, but all boast air conditioning, both hot and cold water, and comfortable, clean surroundings.

Each guest at Monique's has full use of the house, which includes television on the porch, a sitting room, and a small gallery overlooking the lawn and roadway. One communal dining room has shared guest tables, adding an "at home" feel. Home-cooked breakfasts and dinners are provided at reasonable rates. Lunch is not available, but snacks are served on request.

The immaculate and informal guest house offers the use of a nearby swimming pool to its guests, and the innkeepers will happily assist in touring plans. Children under nine years of age sharing with parents are free.

✳

Zollna House
12 Ramlogan Development, LaSeiva, Maraval,
Trinidad, West Indies

Phone: (809) 628–3731
Key: Guest house; 7 units; Inexpensive CP year-round; No credit cards.
Location: 3 mi. to town; 10 mi. to beach; 20 mi. to airport.

Hummingbirds are a few of the beautiful "feathered" visitors who frequent this informal guest house and its gardens, filled with flowering shrubs and coconut, citrus, avocado, and mango trees. The modern, two-storied building with seven guest accommodations and grounds on

Zollna House, Trinidad

several levels offers guests a residential retreat with tranquil views of the harbor.

Zollna House is located on Maraval Valley hillside with not only views of the Gulf of Paria, but also glimpses of the city of Port of Spain. The white structure with black trim is nearly hidden from the road by its surrounding palms and fruit-bearing trees. The seven guest units within are spacious and airy; two offer private baths, with no more than two rooms sharing the oversized common baths. A two bedroom suite with private porch is located on the second floor, where guests will also find two large porches for relaxing, a lounge and television room, a card room, and a refreshment area. A lower floor offers a dining room/lounge and two bedrooms which share a bath.

All meals are available at the Zollna House, with breakfast included in the stay if desired. The optional offerings are varied but have a local flavor, and snacks are available as well. Dinner runs between $8–$10 per person. Guests may also take advantage of a barbecue patio with gardens on the premises.

The guest house provides boardgames and a small library; guests may also walk to a popular night club and restaurant a short distance away. Buses and taxis are also within walking distance, and pretty Maracas Beach is about thirty minutes away by car.

Owners Fred and Barbara Zollna offer many personalized touches to your stay in their affordable "home away from home." All you really "have" to do here is sink down into a hammock and sip a tropical punch while the birds entertain in this small botanical paradise.

❋

Also on the Island

Asa Wright Nature Centre and Lodge

P.O. Box 10, Spring Hill Estate, Arima, Trinidad, West Indies

Phone: (809) 622–7480 in Port-of-Spain

This former coffee, cocoa, and citrus plantation is nestled in a rain forest within a wildlife trust. The conservancy area is also a study facility and refuge and boasts over 100 species of birds, including many rare inhabitants. The Centre is the locale of the annual Audubon Bird

Count each Christmas. The lodge itself is a turn-of-the-century structure with rural warmth and simple accommodations with private baths. Guests here enjoy a homey living room and library, appropriately decorated in bird illustrations, and a dining room with ample, family-style meals. The rain forest surrounding the inn and reserve is lush with not only wildlife, but also fruit and spice trees, ferns, and tall bamboo. Rates with meals included are moderate. Toll-free reservations may be made by phoning Caligo Ventures at (800) 426–7781.

Mount St. Benedict Guest House
Tunapuna, Trinidad, West Indies

Phone: (809) 662–4084

Eight hundred feet above sea level, with views over the Caroni Plain and Piarco Savannah, is a Benedictine monastery; right below it is this peaceful guest house that once served as a religious retreat. The guest house is no longer a part of the monastery, but the hilltop lodging still offers the same solitude and natural beauty that made it an ideal retreat shortly after the turn of the century.

Mount St. Benedict Guest House lies less than ten miles out of Port-of-Spain on a Tunapuna promontory covered with hibiscus and oleander. The guest house is neat and clean and offers fourteen rooms to guests. The rooms have comfortable yet spartan furnishings and sinks with cold water. The shared baths down the hall have hot water for bathing. Though not fancy, the guest accommodations are adequate and definitely restful.

The dining area has picture-window views of the valley and serves simple and ample local food, family style. A living room has comfortable seating. Guests may enjoy this tranquil spot with all meals included for inexpensive rates, which also include a homemade teatime treat.

✳

Tobago

Tobago, 116 square miles in area, is twenty miles to the northeast of Trinidad and can be reached by daily flights from its sister island. This tranquil island is known for its unspoiled beauty—its coconut tree groves, miles of uncrowded beaches, and spectacular underwater reefs.

Togabo, also called the "Robinson Crusoe Island" as the legendary home of the famed character, changed hands repeatedly among the English, Spanish, Dutch, and French and became a pirates' hide-out. In 1762 the British invaded and cleared out the pirates; Tobago later became prosperous as a sugar-producing island.

Scarborough is the chief port and capital of Tobago, with a population of about 17,000. Homes cling to the hillsides and an exotic market takes place here. Fort King George, built in 1777, was constructed on half-hill and half-headland, which it shares with a lighthouse. The Powder Magazine of the fort still stands, as well as the Bell Tank. Scarborough is also home to the Botanic Garden.

The hills of Tobago offer impressive views. Main Ridge runs almost the entire length of the island and reaches 1,800 feet at its highest point, giving dramatic views of bays, coves, and beaches lined with palms, breadfruit, mango, and banana trees. Of the many scenic beaches, Pigeon Point Store Bay, Turtle Beach, and Mount Irvine Bay, which has an eighteen-hole championship golf course, are among the finest.

Nature-lovers may visit the crystal-clear Nylon Pool and Buccoo Reef in Buccoo Bay. Buccoo Reef comprises acres of breathtaking submarine gardens that display many different types of coral in all colors and shapes, various tropical fish, and other creatures, offering a haven for the scuba diver or snorkeler. Non-swimmers can enjoy the scenery through glass-bottomed boats or by wading through the crystal-clear water.

Deep-sea fishing is also famous in Tobago. Kingfish, tarpon, crevalle, sailfish, marlin, wahoo, and bonefish are popular catches.

A special visit from Tobago to the island of "Little Tobago," also known as Ingram's or the Bird of Paradise Island, is worthwhile. Off the northern tip of Tobago, it is the only place outside New Guinea where the birds of paradise exist in their wild state.

✳

Arnos Vale
P.O. Box 208, Scarborough, Tobago, West Indies

Phone: (809) 639–2881
Key: Inn; 30 units; Deluxe/Expensive AP; AE, MC, VI, DC.
Location: On beach; 10 mi. to airport.

This small beach resort sits on a lush 400-acre estate filled with tropical gardens abloom with every possible local flower and quiet paths that lead to nowhere special, but everywhere serene and naturally beautiful. Once a sugar plantation, the inn, submerged in oleander and fragipani, has few remnants of those days intact. The complex on a hill now includes the main house with red roof and stone facade at the top of the hill, a few cottages nestled just above, and the remaining rooms plus informal restaurant on the beach below at Arnos Vale Bay.

The main house has attractive, warm, and comfortable furnishings in its guest lounge and lobby and contains the main dining area on the terrace, with spectacular views of the bay. The English and local cuisine is excellent.

Guestrooms at the inn vary in size and location; a few very nice accommodations are located in the main house, a few are nearby, and the rest are at beach level. All of the guestrooms and suites boast private baths and terraces and are decorated attractively in tropical prints and locally made furniture. Many of the guest accommodations offer superior views of the sea.

In addition to enjoying the picturesque swimming beach, guests may lounge by the swimming pool or use the inn's tennis court (lighted at night).

✳

Blue Waters Inn
Batteaux Bay, Speyside, Tobago, West Indies

Phone: (809) 639–4341
Key: Inn; 28 units; Inexpensive EP year-round; VI, MC, AE, DC.
Location: On beach; 20 mi. to town; 29 mi. to airport.

The Blue Waters Inn received its name more than twenty-five

years ago in honor of the bright blue Atlantic waters that wash up to its sandy shoreline on pretty Batteaux Bay. The informal inn is located in a remote countryside setting on the northeast coast of the island, and its surroundings attract bird watchers from all over who find the property is also a sanctuary for Tobago's many species of rare birds.

Winding country roads through small picturesque towns lead to the hilltop inn, with views of the bay at its feet. The small hotel is formed of simple cabanas that were built in the 1950s as a teenage summer camp. They're simply decorated and have private baths.

The open dining room of the inn, with adjacent bar, serves fixed daily menus, but with advance notice the Zollnas will provide for special dietary requirements. Blue Waters serves breakfast, lunch, dinner, and light snacks.

Besides relaxing in the tranquil surroundings, guests may enjoy fishing, tennis, shuffleboard, scuba, skin diving, and boat trips to Little Tobago arranged by the hospitable hosts.

✳

Della Mira Guest House
P.O. Box 203, Scarborough, Tobago, West Indies

Phone: (809) 639–2531
Key: Guest house; 14 units; Inexpensive/Inexpensive EP; VI, AE, MC.
Location: ¹/₂ mi. to beach; ¹/₂ mi. to town; 8 mi. to airport.

The really special thing about this simple guest house overlooking the sea is its congenial hosts, Neville and Angela Miranda. The 1954-built West Indian home offers a pleasant staff and lots of personal attention to its guests, who stay in the fourteen guestrooms with private baths, hot and cold water, and views of either the sea or the hills and historic Fort King George.

The Della Mira has provided family-style, budget accommodations to the staff of a few movies filmed on the picturesque island, as well as accommodating the Prince of Hungary. The guestrooms and common areas are simply furnished but clean. The living room has a television and small bar for guests, and the guest house lobby is decorated with leafy plants and fresh flowers. The dining room, with white wrought-iron seating and brightly painted walls, has a lovely pool and garden view and serves all three meals, as well as picnic lunches.

The grounds of the guest house are pleasant, the front area with a moon-shaped lawn and tall pine. To the right is the guest house's beauty salon, run by Mrs. Miranda. A flowery hedge gives privacy to the guestrooms fronting the inn, and a rectangular-shaped lawn with flower garden makes up the rear of the grounds. A freshwater swimming pool is set within the garden, and an aviary with a wide variety of local birds is there as well.

Club La Tropicale is adjacent to the guest house; Della Mira's guests have automatic membership in the club with true West Indian ambience. The popular night spot provides dancing and the lively entertainment of steel bands and calypso on weekends. The guest house is situated conveniently fifty yards from the ocean and one-half mile from town.

✳

Also on the Island

Coral Reef Guest House
Milford Road, Tobago, West Indies

Phone: (809) 639–2536

The Coral Reef is a simple, informal guest house about halfway between the airport and the steamer jetty. A short distance away is a pretty coconut-lined beach. The twenty-four guestrooms of the modest guest house are air conditioned, have private baths with hot and cold water, and are sparsely furnished but neat. The small dining room in green and white is airy and serves local dishes. An upstairs sun deck provides panoramic views and an occasional steel band for dancing; a swimming pool is provided on the premises. Double occupancy with breakfast included is inexpensive. Your gracious hostess is Cora Murray.

Mount Irvine Bay Hotel
P.O. Box 222, Tobago, West Indies

Phone: (809) 639–8871
Representative: Robert Reid Associates

On the site of a former sugar mill plantation, this sprawling luxury resort still boasts the old sugar mill that is now an open bar and delightful dining terrace. The tropical landscaped grounds offer sixty-four guestrooms in a two-story building overlooking the sea and the professional golf course, as well as twenty-three cottages around the grounds. All of the accommodations are attractively decorated in contemporary furnishings and coordinating tropical prints. The carpeted rooms feature modern, private baths and relaxing terraces. The cottages offer two-bedroom suites with private patios. The hotel has a lovely pool with a swim-up bar alongside the Sugar Mill Restaurant, an adjoining eighteen-hole golf course (guests play at reduced fees), two tennis courts (with lights), a shopping arcade, and a palm-shaded beach with bar. Rates are expensive during off-season and deluxe on-season EP.

Netherlands Antilles and Aruba

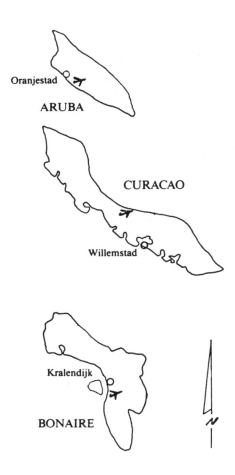

Oranjestad

ARUBA

CURACAO

Willemstad

Kralendijk

BONAIRE

N

Not far off the coast of Venezuela lie the three "ABC" islands—Aruba, Bonaire, and Curacao—that constitute the southern complement of the Netherlands or Dutch Antilles Islands, with the exception of Aruba. Aruba separated from the Netherlands Antilles in January 1986 and is now autonomous. The other Caribbean Dutch islands of Saba, St. Eustatius, and St. Maarten form what is called the Dutch Windward Islands.

These three small islands reflect their Dutch heritage in the interesting eighteenth-century architecture and old-world charm that abounds, in contrast to the modern gambling casinos and popular international shopping also there. Dutch is the official language of the islands, but the local dialect of "Papiamento" is most prevalent in these islands. The dialect evolves primarily from Spanish, Dutch, Portuguese, and some English, and French. Most of the population also speak English and Spanish.

The currency of the three islands is the Netherlands Antillean guilder or florin. U.S. dollars and credit cards are also accepted widely. The electrical voltage on the islands is the same or compatible with U.S. appliances. The Netherlands Antilles are on Atlantic Standard Time all year. When the East Coast is on Daylight Saving Time, the time is the same in both locations.

The government of Bonaire and Curacao is the same as that of the Dutch Windwards, the five islands collectively forming the Netherlands Antilles and being members of the Kingdom of the Netherlands. The Queen is the sovereign of the Kingdom and is represented by a Governor appointed by her. As mentioned above, Aruba is now self-governing.

❇

Aruba

Aruba is the most western of the Leeward group of these islands and measures 19.6 miles long and six miles wide. The dry climate, with only twenty inches of rain per year, and the always sunny skies yield only a slight change in the 83-degree weather from day to night. This dry, almost arid climate gives Aruba, as well as her two sister islands, unusual Caribbean scenery. A wide variety of cacti, rock formations, and trade wind–sculpted Watapana trees create an Arizona-type landscape. The southwest coast of the island offers seven miles of pure white beach, lined with palms and bathed by calm, clear blue-green water. The northeast coast, on the other hand, is characterized by wild waves and a natural coral bridge carved by the sea's on-going rage.

After its discovery in 1499, Aruba was a part of the swashbuckling pirate era that followed. The Dutch ultimately took control of the island in 1816, and in 1824 gold was discovered, bringing riches to the island until about 1913. Evidence of the Gold Rush days is found in the abandoned mines that dot the sagebrushed countryside. Actually, it was "black gold," or oil, that made Aruba prosperous. After the oil was discovered in 1924, Exxon soon established a refinery on the island.

Regular flights arrive daily in Aruba from the United States, and connections are available from South American, Puerto Rico, and the Dominican Republic, among other destinations. U.S. citizens need to show proof of identity in the form of a birth certificate, passport, or voter's registration card and must pay a nominal departure tax. Cruise ships serve the island regularly, and tourism is a large industry on Aruba. Getting around the island can be done by bus, taxi, or rental car. Buses run daily between town and hotels, and taxis with fixed rates are available. Most American car rental agencies are represented, and only a valid U.S. license is required. Driving here is American-style, to the right.

Aruba's capital city, Oranjestad, offers some Dutch architecture, an active harbor, and a few historic sights, such as Fort Zoutman and the William III Tower. But the capital town attracts most visitors because of its almost duty-free shopping. Merchandise imported from South America and all over the world, as well as local handicrafts, is for sale in the many shops, with no sales tax charged and almost no duty. The Watapana Festival held here every Tuesday night is a colorful market place with local, reasonable island handicrafts and native foods for sale.

Exploring other parts of the island reveals that Aruba has some fine beaches, among those Eagle Beach and Palm Beach, that are characterized by white sands and turquoise waters and the contrasting hotel-casinos that line the shore. Driving through the *cunucu* or countryside, the visitor will view modest, colorful homes with small, well-kept tropical gardens that are set against a background of windswept divi divi (or Watapana) trees, cacti and rocks.

Along with viewing the Natural Bridge on the windward coast, the visitor will see the unusual rock formations of Ayo and Casibari as well as the coves of Andicouri, Dos Playa, Boca Prins and Frenchman's Pass and the sand dunes of California and Prins. The cliff-perched Pirate's Castle at Bushiribana on the windward coast is a deserted gold mill, similar to the one found in the ghost town of Balashi. The village of Noord is known for St. Ann's Church, with its hand-carved seventeenth-century Dutch altar.

The calm, clear waters of Aruba make all water sports inviting and popular. Palm Beach is one of the safest swimming spots around. Sailing trips are available on catamarans; deep-sea charter boats can be rented for the day or half of the day. Although Aruba has no professional golf courses, the Aruba Golf Club offers an unusual course with oiled sand greens.

Aruba's Las Vegas-type strip has five casinos with gambling and live entertainment, as well as several local nightclubs, discos, and dancing spots. Restaurants range from local Aruban establishments to fast food to fine eateries. The food choices are international with an emphasis on Chinese and French.

For additional information on Aruba contact:

Aruba Tourist Authority
521 Fifth Avenue
New York, NY 10017
(212) 246–3030

❋

The Edge's, Aruba

The Edge's
L. G. Smith Boulevard 458, Oranjestad, Aruba

Phone: (011–297) 8–21072; (800) 252–1070

The Edge's is a well-known "windsurfing hotel" on the island. There are thirty-eight apartments, some facing the sea, others with courtyard views. Several windsurfing packages are available.

✻

The Vistalmar
Becutiweg 28, Aruba

Phone: (011–297) 8–47737
Key: Guest house; 8 units; Inexpensive EP year-round; No credit cards.
Location: On sea; 1 mi. to town; 2 mi. to airport.

When Aruban Alby Yarzagaray decided he would like to do something for the tourists who visited his land, he came up with the Vistalmar: an intimate assemblage of accommodations that convey the warmth and quality of home, yet within budget prices. He worked

The Vistalmar, Aruba

alongside the construction crew for three years and in January 1980 opened his guest house, offering eight units housed in twin two-story buildings with peaked roofs overlooking the Caribbean sea.

Both Alby and his gracious wife Katy are involved in every aspect of the operation, including providing some special homebaked breads to go along with the first morning complimentary breakfast foods guests will find in their refrigerator.

The guest accommodations at Vistalmar include efficiencies, one-bedroom apartments, and two- or three-bedroom villas. Each of the well-maintained units offers a complete kitchen, with attractive tile decor, toaster oven, microwave, picnic cooler, blender, and quality dishware. The spacious bedrooms in the one-bedroom units offer a king size bed or two double beds, and all units boast nicely coordinated bedspreads and draperies and a private bathroom with combination tub/shower, as well as a separate dressing room. The living rooms are comfortably furnished with pretty print sofas and chairs and special touches, such as Oriental rugs and fresh flower arrangements. Guest accommodations also offer large sun porches equipped with chaises and chairs and, more importantly, spectacular views of the sea just 100 yards ahead. Telephones and satellite televisions are also supplied in each unit.

For families traveling with small children, the Vistalmar offers some special hospitality in the form of baby beds, play pens, high chairs, and strollers available upon request. A convenient laundry is located on the premises.

A pier for small boats was added in recent years, as well as a sandy area for sunbathing even though the guest house is not on a beachy stretch. Some unique steps formed from coral and lined in rocks from around the island lead to the water. The guest house offers watersports facilities, including paddleboats, and guests have use of bicycles and snorkel gear. A pretty garden surrounds the Vistalmar, as well as picturesque palms, giving it a private feel in this quiet residential area. For those wishing to explore the island without a car, a bus stop is located right at the door of the Vistalmar.

✳

Curacao

This island thirty-five miles off the coast of Venezuela is a miniature Holland, boasting the most interesting architecture in the West

Indies. The Dutch influence on the thirty-seven-mile-long by seven-mile wide Curacao goes back to the mid-1600s, when the island was ruled by the Dutch Stuyvesant; the numerous forts and ramparts that protected the island are still evident. In 1915 one of the largest oil refineries was built here, turning the sleepy island into a teeming work and living place, with Curacao becoming the most populated island of the Netherlands Antilles.

The countryside, reflecting the island's dry, sunny climate, offers desert scenery distinguished by three-pronged cactus, aloes, and the divi divi trees molded by the trade winds. Dutch windmills, used for irrigation, are seen all over.

Daily flights from the United States arrive in Curacao, and connections are available to other parts of the Caribbean and South America. U.S. visitors need only proof of citizenship in the form of a passport, birth certificate, or voter's registration card and must pay a small departure tax. Curacao is a popular cruise shop port; inter-island flights between Curacao, Aruba, Bonaire, and St. Maarten are available. Also, a special ferry boat service departs each Tuesday from Curacao bound for Aruba.

Getting around the island can be achieved by taxis that carry official rate sheets according to destination, by bus, by sightseeing taxis and buses, or by car rental. Good roads (with driving on the right side) and international signs make renting a car a good option here, and the major car rental agencies are represented.

The "storybook" village of Willemstad is not only the capital of Curacao, but also the government seat of the Netherlands Antilles. An unusual pedestrian bridge, Queen Emma, connects the two sides of the city, which has grown on both sides of the picturesque canal. The bridge swings open more than thirty times a day for ships that pass. The immaculate streets of Willemstad are lined with 200-year-old houses in bright pastels with steep gables and red-tiled roofs. A walking tour of the old "European" city provides a remarkable selection of low-duty, international shopping, as well as many reminders of its history. The Mikve Israel Synagogue, with its fascinating Dutch Colonial architecture, is located in the heart of town. Dating from 1732, it is the oldest synagogue in the Western Hemisphere. Fort Amsterdam, the site of the Governor's Palace and the 1769 Dutch Reformed Church, is also set in the Colonial town. Near the bridge is the Floating Market, a colorful display of docked boats from Venezuela and other Caribbean islands selling tropical fruits, vegetables, and more. Fort Nassau on a hilltop offers great views of the town and houses an unusual restaurant built within the old ramparts.

The countryside or *cunucu* of Curacao displays towering cacti and rolling hills topped by historic plantation houses. Going east, the visitor can view the Amstel Brewery (the only beer in the world brewed from salt water) and the Curacao Liqueur Distillery, as well as the botanical garden and zoo. Groot St. Joris is a coconut grove northeast of town where coconuts may be personally selected and then opened on the spot. Spanish Water, also to the east, is a popular water sport and yachting spot.

On the northwestern end of Curacao is the 4,500-acre Christoffel Park, which is home to many unusual plants and trees (including rare orchids, divi divi trees, and sabal palms), Curacao deer, and a wide variety of birds, and 1,239-foot Mt. Christoffel. Near here the Ascension Plantation, a typical restored landhuis (plantation house), is open to the public the first Sunday of each month.

The city of Willemstad becomes almost magical at night, as soft lights illuminate the enchanting roof lines of the Dutch buildings and more dramatic lights overhang the main streets. Four casinos, several discos, international restaurants, and some local "folkloric" shows are there for the enjoying. Many of the restaurants offer unique dining ambience, such as a historic landhuis with Dutch and colonial antiques or an ancient fort turned bistro with dark wood beams and stone walls. Popular dishes include "stuffed cheeses" and the Dutch adopted Indonesian delicacy, Rijsttafel, offered in some special dining establishments.

For more information on Curacao contact:

Curacao Tourist Board
400 Madison Avenue, Suite 311
New York, NY 10017
(212) 751–8266

✳

Avila Beach Hotel
Penstraat 130–134, P.O. Box 791, Willemstad, Curacao, Netherlands Antilles

Phone: (011–599) 9–614377
Key: Historic inn; 45 units; Expensive/Inexpensive EP; AE, DC, MC, VI.
Location: On beach; 1 mi. to town; 10 mi. to airport.

This gracious, mustard-yellow colonial inn offers the best of what picturesque Curacao has to offer: architectural beauty, local charm and history, personal service, a secluded beachside location walking distance to town, and ultra-modern facilities. In other words, the Avila Beach Hotel gives the traveler a very close look at the real Curacao without sacrificing comfort and does so at very reasonable prices.

The Avila Beach consists of two buildings, both built in the colonial style. The older, two-story structure was built around 1780. This mansion was historically known as the Belle Alliance and served as a residence of Curacao governors between 1812 and 1828. It was converted to a hotel in 1949 and purchased by the present owner and director, Mr. F. N. Moller, in 1977. A gracious and enthusiastic host, Mr. Moller is a native of Denmark who has lived in the Netherlands Antilles since 1960. A major remodeling program has recently been completed at the Avila Beach under his direction.

Driving up to the hotel, just a few minutes out of downtown Willemstad, you'll notice other mansions of similar vintage, though not so well restored. The pretty Dutch colonial with white pillars and trim and small balconies under the upper windows is stately behind the circular drive bordered by well-manicured gardens.

The spacious lobby, used often for musical events and art exhibits, has attractive gold ceramic tile, rattan furnishings, a polished piano, wood-beamed ceilings, and arched doorways. Lots of fresh flowers, overhead fans, brass lamp sconces filling the room with soft light, original Curacao watercolors, and classical background music set the tone for this relaxing and charming spot. A small conference or banquet room (one of two offered) is located off the lobby area.

The lobby opens onto a quiet patio area that leads to the hotel's beach area and restaurant and bar. Miniature turn-of-the-century lampposts are scattered about here between the palms and planter-enclosed gardens. The bar, shaped like a schooner, overlooks the sea, as does the Belle Terrace restaurant of the hotel, with split-level dining. Tiny lights are hung from the pretty arbor above the restaurant's outside eating terrace. The Belle Terrace offers reasonable Scandinavian and local cuisine, with an emphasis on fresh fish. Lunch and dinner are offered here along with a breakfast buffet served from 7:00 to 10:00 A.M. each morning.

Lounge chairs with tables for refreshments and thatched umbrellas for shade are positioned comfortably around the hotel's own small and protected beach that provides a pleasant and safe swimming or sunning spot. Large beach towels are provided at the front desk for guests' use. Also, a small sundry store is conveniently located on the back patio area.

While the Dutch and Curacao architecture has been carefully preserved on the exterior of the buildings, the guestrooms at the hotel have been totally refurbished and reflect a Scandinavian-modern decor. The contrasts are surprisingly pleasing and, as Mr. Moller explains, very practical. The sleek, neat look of the guestrooms includes polished tile floors, crisp white walls, built-ins hung off the floor for maximum cleanliness, and air conditioning. The attractive decor has a different look in each of the individually designed rooms that are, likewise, all different in size and form. The windows are covered with a pretty striped canvas covering and original watercolors grace the walls of the rooms; some boast ocean views. All of the guestrooms have private, modern baths.

Despite the size of the Avila Beach Hotel, it manages to convey the hospitality usually found in establishments much smaller. Its staff and management work hard to make it a relaxing, family-style hotel with a lot of repeat business.

✳

Bonaire

The coral-reef island of Bonaire, five miles wide and twenty-four miles long, offers an uncrowded alternative to touring the "ABC's." The desert-like landscape is notable for housing the beautiful flamingo, as well as 145 other species of birds, in its southern area with a salt lake.

The island's brilliant blue-green water and sugar-white sand are matched by the brilliantly-colored tropical fish that abound. This fact, along with water visibility topping one hundred feet, makes it a haven for scuba and snorkeling aficionados. Note that the preservation-minded islanders do not allow spearfishing or coral collecting.

Bonaire was discovered in 1499 by the Spanish; the Dutch arrived in 1634. Salt mining eventually became a major industry on the island, and its production re-emerged in the 1960s, along with tourism.

The island is a fifteen-minute airplane hop from Curacao, and a nominal departure tax is levied. Taxis with established rates are available, as are rental cars; driving is on the right side. No public bus system exists, but sightseeing bus and taxi tours are available.

Besides water sports and bird-viewing, visitors might opt for a cruise to the uninhabited island of Klein Bonaire for a picnic and beach excursion. Touring around Bonaire might include a visit to the capital, Kralendijk. This small Dutch town is bathed in pastel shades and offers some shopping bargains. The bay city has two churches worth viewing, as well as the Instituto Folklore Bonaire with museum offerings. Fort Oranje here has an ancient cannon intact.

North and inland from the capital is Gotomeer, the location of a salt lake and some flamingos. Washington/Slagbaai National Park at the northern end of the island is a 13,500-acre game preserve with over 130 species of birds. Nestled in this cactus forest with coral rock formations are two lakes that are popular with flamingos, and an excellent snorkeling beach, Playa Foenchi.

The southern section of Bonaire is made up of salt flats with the largest accessible flamingo nesting and breeding grounds in the world. Primitive stone huts once used by the salt workers/slaves have been rebuilt here by the government. The 1837-built lighthouse, Willemstoren, is on the way south from here to Lac Bay, an excellent reef-protected swimming and snorkeling spot.

For more information on Bonaire contact:

Bonaire Tourist Information Office
c/o Resorts Management
201¹/₂ East 29th Street
New York, NY 10016
(212) 779–0242

❋

Carib Inn
JA Abraham Boulevard 46, Bonaire,
Netherlands Antilles

Phone: (011–599) 7–8819
Key: Guest house; 9 units; Inexpensive/Inexpensive EP; AE, MC, VI.
Location: On beach; near town; 1 mi. to airport.

Bonaire's attraction as a diving locale makes this small inn's appeal especially inviting to diving aficionados. Located on the premises of the Carib Inn is its own dive shop, with a full selection of gear for sale and rental equipment. The inn's dive boats dock right at the private pier, and special reef trips to exclusive sites are offered. When weather permits, the inn takes guests with a lot of experience on "wreck" diving expeditions.

Built as a private house in 1968, the Carib Inn was converted in 1979 to an intimate dive resort by Bruce Bowker, the owner and personal host at Carib Inn. The economy-minded rooms have shared baths and overlook the swimming pool and patio. Two large upstairs rooms can form a suite and offer a balcony with ocean views. Maid service is offered Monday through Friday. Although no meals are offered at the inn, kitchenettes with refrigerators and electric kettles are available. Restaurants and shops are within walking distance.

Bruce Bowker personally runs the informal inn, giving each guest his attention and knowledge of the area, especially his diving experience.

✳

Reservation Representatives

American Wolfe International
1890 Palmer Avenue
Larchmont, NY 10538
(914) 833–3303; (800) 223–5695

Caribbean Inns Ltd.
P.O. Box 7411
Hilton Head Island, SC 29938
(803) 686–7411; (800) 633–7411

David B. Mitchell & Company, Inc.
200 Madison Avenue
New York, NY 10016
(212) 696–1323; (800) 372–1323

Flagship Hotels & Resorts
43 Kensico Drive
Mt. Kisco, NY 10549
(800) 235–3505 or 729–3524

International Travel & Resorts, Inc.
4 Park Avenue
New York, NY 10016
(212) 545–8469; (800) 223–9815

Jacques de Larsay
622 Broadway
New York, NY 10012
(212) 477–1600; (800) 366–1510

Jane Martin
2170 Broadway
Suite 3317
New York, NY 10024
(212) 319–7488

Leading Hotels of the World
747 Third Avenue
New York, NY 10017–2847
(212) 838–3110; (800) 223–6800

Mondotels
1500 Broadway, Suite 1101
New York, NY 10036
(212) 719–5750; (800) 847–4249

Preferred Hotels
1901 South Meyers Road
Oakbrook Terrace, IL 60181
(800) 323–7500

Ralph Locke Islands
P.O. Box 800
Waccabuc, NY 10597
(800) 223–1108

Rawlins Plantation
111 Charles Street
Boston, MA 02114
(617) 367–8959

Ray Morrow Associates
360 Main Street
Ridgefield, CT 06877
(203) 697–2340; (800) 223–9838

Resorts Management, Inc.
The Carriage House
201½ East 29th Street
New York, NY 10016
(212) 696–4566; (800) 225–4255

Robert Reid Associates
500 Plaza Drive
Secaucus, NJ 07096
(201) 902–7878; (800) 223–6517

Rockresorts
501 East El Camino Real
Boca Raton, FL 33432
(800) 223–7637

Unique Vacations
7610 SW 61st Avenue
Miami, FL 33143
(800) SANDALS

WIMCO
Box 1461
Newport, RI 02840
(401) 849–8012; (800) 932–3222

Indexes

Alphabetical Index

Inns with Guest Kitchens

Inns Near Towns

Romantic Inns

Secluded, Peaceful Inns

Inns That Do Not Allow Smoking